R

THE Holocaust

Editor
Geoffrey Wigoder

A
Grolier Student
Library

Volume 4
Tehran Children to Zyklon B

Grolier Educational
SHERMAN TURNPIKE, DANBURY, CONNECTICUT

t and Editorial Advisor

les E. Smith

aging Editor

chel Gilon

Library of Congress Cataloging-in-Publication Data

The Holocaust.
     p.   cm.
     Summary. Articles identify and describe individuals and events
connected with the persecution of Jews and others across Europe in
the 1930s and 1940s.
     ISBN 0-7172-7637-6
     1. Holocaust , Jewish (1939-1945)—Encyclopedias, Juvenile.
     [1. Holocaust , Jewish (1939-1945)—Encyclopedias.]
     D804.25.H65   1996
     940.53'18'03—dc20   96-9566
                                                                    CIP
                                                                    AC

Published 1997 by Grolier Educational,
Sherman Turnpike, Danbury, Connecticut
© 1997 by Charles E. Smith Books, Inc.

Set ISBN 0-7172-7637-6
Volume 4: ISBN 0-7172-7641-4

For information, address the publisher:
Grolier Educational, Sherman Turnpike, Danbury, Connecticut 06816

Cover design by Smart Graphics
Planned and produced by The Jerusalem Publishing House, Jerusalem
Printed in Hong Kong

t

TEHRAN CHILDREN

Polish Jewish CHILDREN taken to PALESTINE in February 1943 via Tehran, Iran. Most of them were between the ages of 12 and 15. They had escaped to SOVIET RUSSIA in 1939, together with their families, just before the advance of the German forces. Once in Soviet Russia, the families were deported to FORCED LABOR CAMPS. They were subjected to terrible suffering and most of the parents and siblings died of starvation and disease. In other cases, parents and children were separated and lost contact.

In 1942, under the terms of a Polish-Soviet agreement, between 12,000 and 20,000 Polish children were allowed to leave Soviet Russia. However, as the Polish and Soviet authorities often prevented JEWS from leaving the country and almost half of these children were Jewish, only 861 Jewish children, most of them orphans, arrived in the fall of 1942 in Iran. After taking some time to recover, the children were taken to Palestine. They received a joyous reception on their arrival in February 1943. Most were absorbed into kibbutzim (communal settlements).

TENENBAUM, MORDECHAI

(1916–1943) A leader of the VILNA, WARSAW and BIALYSTOK UNDERGROUND fighters during WORLD WAR II. In 1938, he joined the staff of the Zionist Youth head office in Warsaw, POLAND. In September 1939, he and his comrades left Warsaw for Vilna, Lithuania, hoping to reach PALESTINE. The British were limiting Jewish immigration to Palestine. Since not enough

"Tehran Children" arriving in Atlit, Palestine at the end of their journey

immigration certificates were available, he obtained forged documents for many Zionist youth that allowed them to escape. Out of a sense of duty, however, Tenenbaum himself decided to remain in Vilna.

The possession of work permits saved Jews from death during the mass murders of June 1941 in Vilna, and Tenenbaum provided many such false permits to Zionist youth. The leaders of the Zionist Youth Movement decided that its members should be moved to Bialystok, where the situation was somewhat better. With forged documents, he left Vilna for Grodno and Bialystok in Belarus, where he organized armed undergrounds. Returning to Warsaw, he declared at a meeting of various Jewish political groups that the massacre at Vilna was a sign of the planned destruction of Europe's Jews.

Tenenbaum was one of the founders of the short-lived united armed underground in Warsaw. He visited Zionist Youth Movement branches in different ghettos, obtaining information and working with

Mordechai Tenenbaum

RESISTANCE leaders. In 1942, he became a founder of the Warsaw underground, the JEWISH FIGHTING ORGANIZATION.

Returning to Bialystok, he learned that the Germans had sealed off the ghetto. Later, he managed to enter and unify the ghetto's underground movement. He appealed to the Polish underground to supply weapons and to the Western world to save the remaining Jews of Poland. A large deportation of Jews from Bialystok, in February 1943, led to a decision to first fight in the ghetto and then escape to the forest. He became the commander of the underground in July and on 16 August 1943 launched an uprising. The German forces surrounding the ghetto overpowered the fighters and ruined the plan to break out. His exact fate is unknown. He may have fallen in battle or committed suicide.

TESTIMONIES

The first histories of the HOLOCAUST were largely based on records kept by the Germans (see HISTORIOGRAPHY OF THE HOLOCAUST). While the Germans recorded almost every detail of their activities in writing and on film, the Jewish internal experience was almost unknown. Jews in the PARTISAN groups, the UNDERGROUND, and the CAMPS had few opportunities to maintain records. After the war, DIARIES and other writings did come to light. However, to build a full picture of the Holocaust, the writings made during the Holocaust have been supplemented by recording the experiences and stories of as many survivors as possible since the end of WORLD WAR II.

The first attempt at documentation was made by the CENTRE DE DOCUMENTATION JUIVE CONTEMPORAINE, which began to collect material in Grenoble, FRANCE, during the war. After the war, it continued its work in Paris. In 1945, the Central Historical Commission in Munich collected memoirs and eye-witness accounts from various DISPLACED PERSONS CAMPS in GERMANY, ITALY and AUSTRIA. These were published in a journal used in the TRIALS OF WAR CRIMINALS at Nuremberg. To add to the written memoirs available, the practice of oral documentation began to be widely used in the late 1950s. This was made easier by the recent invention of the portable tape recorder. At the same time, YAD VASHEM opened a department to record as many survivors as possible telling their stories. The Oral History department of the Hebrew University was a pioneer in subject-oriented oral documentation—that is, testimonies recorded as part of research projects and seen as supplementing the written documentation. This approach is based on the understanding that although testimonies are valuable, memory on its own cannot be relied upon, especially as the time gap lengthens. In the course of time, "oral history" of the Holocaust was being recorded in many academic institutions as well as communities around the world.

In the 1980s, an extra dimension was added: the video camera. A project at Yale University videotaped Holocaust survivors, with attention to both historical and psychological aspects of their stories. The video interview has now become widely adopted. Film producer Steven Spielberg gave a large part of the profit from his film *Schindler's List* (see SCHINDLER, OSKAR) to a project for videotaping as many survivors as possible, under the guidance of the UNITED STATES HOLOCAUST MEMORIAL MUSEUM in Wash-

ington D.C. and other institutions. The importance of these testimonies, recorded 50 years after the Holocaust, is not so much for new historical research as it is for their educational potential, especially for future generations. As the generation of the Holocaust comes to an end, it is invaluable that these personal experiences be recorded on video. Moreover, the authenticity of these testimonies will provide a challenge to HOLOCAUST DENIAL when there are no longer living witnesses to give testimony.

THERESIENSTADT (Terezin)

Town and army barracks near PRAGUE in CZECHOSLOVAKIA, converted by the Nazis into a Jewish GHETTO.

When the Nazi rulers of the Protectorate of BOHEMIA AND MORAVIA began to separate Jews from Gentiles, the town of Theresienstadt became a site for concentrating Jews. In November 1941, the first Czech Jews were deported to Theresienstadt. Within six months, one-third of the Protectorate's

Entrance to Theresienstadt

From the Nazi film of Theresienstadt, staged to make the concentration camp look like a place of recreation

JEWS had been concentrated there—some 28,000 people. The ghetto was run by the Germans and guarded by Czech police.

The Nazis always tried to hide their anti-Jewish brutality from the world. They chose to make Theresienstadt a "model" CONCENTRATION CAMP to be used to deceive the world about the true nature of their plans for Europe's Jews. It was depicted by the Nazis as a "comfortable" ghetto, even a "Ghetto Paradise." They even made a film showing Theresienstadt as a sort of holiday camp. Czech, and later German and Austrian Jews, were encouraged to accept DEPORTATION to this "independent" Jewish community, where the Nazis claimed that normal family life was possible. In particular, the Germans sought to place privileged Jews in Theresienstadt—the famous, the wealthy, and war veterans. Before their deportation, German and Austrian Jews signed contracts exchanging property and wealth for family apartments in Theresienstadt. Upon their arrival, the Jews quickly discovered that these agreements were meaningless.

In July 1942, all non-Jews were evicted from the town to make room for more Jews. By September, 53,000 Jews were crowded inside the ghetto. In the coming months and years, Jews from DENMARK, HUNGARY, LUXEMBOURG, the NETHERLANDS, and POLAND were sent to the ghetto. In total, 141,000 Jews entered Theresienstadt.

Conditions there were as dreadful as those in other ghettos and concentration camps. The Jews were forced to live in overcrowded apartments and makeshift dormitories. The lack of living space and hygienic facilities led to widespread disease, which was made worse by the lack of food. More than 33,000 Jews died of malnutrition, typhus, and other illnesses. In 1942, the death rate was so high that a crematorium that could handle 200 bodies a day was built. The residents lived in constant fear of arrest, brutality, and deportation to an unknown destination. Gradually, inmates were deported to DEATH CAMPS—mostly to AUSCHWITZ. Of the 80,000 Jews sent to death camps, only some 3,000 survived.

The ghetto's main Jewish leader was Jacob EDELSTEIN, a socialist Zionist from Bohemia. As chief of the Council of Elders (see JUDENRAT), he tried to pro-

Memorial at Theresienstadt

vide some aspects of normal life to comfort the population of the ghetto. The council was forced to take responsibility for providing food and housing to the residents, and even to supply the Nazis with deportation lists. Yet education of the ghetto's youth was given top priority. Although education was technically forbidden, regular classes were held for the young, often taught by Zionist youth movement leaders. Religious services were organized. The council also ran opera, orchestra, and theater performances. The optimism of these activities, which was an important form of RESISTANCE to the Nazis' inhumanity, is perhaps the most powerful memory of Theresienstadt.

The "normal" life the Jews made for themselves also gave the Nazis a rare opportunity to disguise their treatment of the Jews and to claim that Theresienstadt was a comfortable, independent community. They even printed stamps and paper money bearing the ghetto's name (and the portrait of Edelstein) to prove the ghetto's independence. Inmates were allowed to correspond with relatives and friends—on the condition that they did not tell the truth about life and the physical conditions in the ghetto.

The Nazis won a propaganda victory in July 1944, when the SS hosted a delegation from the International RED CROSS in Theresienstadt. Before the visit, a cafe and shops were built, gardens were planted, and inmates were briefed about how to behave in the presence of the visitors. To reduce the obvious overcrowding, the SS deported a number of Jews before the visit. The Red Cross delegation was successfully deceived.

When the ghetto was liberated by the Red Army on 8 May 1945, over 17,000 Jews were found still alive, but suffering from diseases. After the war, articles hidden by Jews in the ghetto were found. In particular, hundreds of drawings by artists and children were discovered, providing a silent account of life in Theresienstadt. These drawings are currently on display at the Jewish Museum in Prague. Today, the army barracks of Theresienstadt are the site of a memorial for the many Jews and non-Jews who were held or killed there by the Nazis. The crematorium and cemetery can be visited.

THIERACK, OTTO GEORG

(1889–1946) Nazi lawyer. Thierack served as Germany's President of the People's Court (1936–1942) and then as Minister of Justice (1942–1945).

He received his law degree in 1914 and served as a lieutenant in World War I. After the war, he became a public prosecutor in Leipzig (1921) and Dresden (1926). Thierack joined the NAZI PARTY in 1932. From 1933, he served as the Nazi minister of justice for the German state of Saxony. There he led the Nazi effort to drive JEWS and political opponents out of jobs in the court system. In 1935, Thierack was appointed vice-president of the Supreme Court in Leipzig. One year later, Adolf HITLER chose him to head the People's Court in BERLIN.

In 1942, Thierack became Reich Minister of Justice. He transformed the court system into an instrument of terror and repression. He set guidelines for the interpretation of Nazi laws and the sentencing of defendants. Furthermore, he constantly transferred prisoners, especially Jews and GYPSIES, from German prisons to the SS for "extermination through work."

The Allies arrested Thierack after WORLD WAR II. He committed suicide in November 1946, shortly before his trial.

THIRD REICH

("Third Empire")

Term used to denote the Nazi regime in GERMANY. It springs from the idea that the medieval German Empire was the First Empire and the united German Empire of 1871–1918 was the Second. The Third Reich was established by the Nazis and lasted from 1933 to 1945.

TISO, JOZEF

(1887–1947) Pro-Nazi politician and Catholic priest who ruled SLOVAKIA from 1939 to 1945. Tiso studied to be a Catholic priest and was ordained in 1910. The young Tiso was a Slovak nationalist and, after the establishment of a united CZECHOSLOVAKIA in 1918, he called for the separation of Slovakia into an independent state. He was a member of parliament from 1920, and was minister of public health during 1927–1929.

Tiso moved up in the ranks of the Slovak People's Party until he reached the position of premier of the Slovak Autonomous Government in 1938. Then he began to prepare ANTI-JEWISH LEGISLATION.

In March 1939, Tiso proclaimed an independent Slovak republic of which he was premier until Octo-

Otto Georg Thierack

Jozef Tiso

ber 1939, when he became president. He held that post throughout WORLD WAR II. In August 1939, JEWS were excluded from the universities and the professions.

Tiso's goal was to have a Slovakia without Jews. ANTISEMITISM became the official government policy in late 1941. He quickly agreed to Germany's demand to deport Jews to POLAND. His only condition was that the Jews' property be left for the Slovaks, and not confiscated by the Germans. His policies were repeatedly condemned by the Vatican.

Tiso was placed on the Allies' list of war criminals and in April 1945, he fled to a monastery in AUSTRIA. In June of that year, he was arrested by American Army authorities, who turned him over to the newly restored Czechoslovakia. He was tried, condemned to death in April 1947, and hanged. He is still admired by some Slovak nationalists.

TODT ORGANIZATON

see ORGANIZATION TODT.

TOUVIER, PAUL

(1915–1995) Chief of the VICHY militia, based in Lyon, FRANCE. Touvier was a close associate of the GESTAPO chief in Lyon, Klaus BARBIE.

After France was liberated in 1944, there was a purge of COLLABORATORS. Paul Touvier was twice sentenced to death in his absence, for his role in the Vichy militia's persecution of JEWS and RESISTANCE workers. However, through the years, Touvier managed to avoid being captured. This was due to the protection given him by the French Catholic Church. In 1971, the French President Georges Pompidou officially pardoned Touvier. (Pompidou wished to finally bring to a close the memory of the Vichy years).

Even so, in 1992, the case against Touvier was reopened. On 4 April 1994, Touvier became the first French citizen ever to be convicted of CRIMES AGAINST HUMANITY. He was found to be responsible for the revenge killings of seven Jews in June 1944. The conviction showed that the French courts were finally ready to recognize the role of the Vichy government in the "FINAL SOLUTION." His punishment was life imprisonment.

TRANSNISTRIA

Today a province of the Republic of Moldova—formerly part of BESSARABIA. Transnistria belonged to ROMANIA at the start of WORLD WAR II, when 340,000 JEWS were living there—10 percent of Romania's population.

Under the terms of the NAZI-SOVIET PACT (23 August 1939), the area was given to SOVIET RUSSIA, which divided it between the Socialist Republics of Moldova and UKRAINE. In June 1941, GERMANY attacked Soviet Russia. Germany conquered Transnistria and handed it back to its ally, Romania. Romanian armies accused the Jews of Transnistria of having assisted Soviet troops during the bitter fighting and executed a number of them. Many Jews managed to flee the area before the arrival of German troops. However, tens of thousands of Jews were murdered in the first months of occupation by EINSATZGRUPPEN and by German and Romanian soldiers.

The Romanian ruler, Marshal Ion ANTONESCU, stated that the Jews were an "enemy population." He decided to deport all the Jews of Bessarabia, BUKOVINA, and northern Moldova to Transnistria. Lack of organization, combined with the strong ANTISEMITISM among the Romanian armies, turned the transportation of about 120,000 Jews in 1941–1942 into a deadly ordeal. After being deprived of their personal possessions, thousands were packed into freight trains without food or water and many died. Others were forced to make the long journey in a DEATH MARCH, with the weak and sick dying along the way. In both groups, a number of people were shot at random by soldiers.

Survivors told of dead bodies being stripped of all their clothes and belongings and left lying on the ground. Another 30,000 persons were deported to Transnistria from Romania for political reasons; a majority of them were Jews. Many more slaughters were carried out by Romanians, Germans, Ukrainians, and the local population. In Transnistria the Jews were herded into CAMPS and GHETTOS and subjected to FORCED LABOR. During the first winter (1941–1942), tens of thousands died from starvation and the typhus epidemic, which swept through the camps. Though local Jews tried to help the newcomers, 90,000 of the 150,000 deportees died in Transnistria. Jewish organizations in Romania tried to assist their brethren in Transnistria and

Drawing by Arnold Degan: "Entrance to camp" in Transnistria, 1942. The sign says "Juden Lager"—Jews' camp

even obtained official authorization to do so. Toward the beginning of the winter of 1942, food and

medical supplies sent by Romanian Jews and by Jewish organizations abroad were reaching the de-

Deportation of Jews from Bessarabia to Transnistria, 1941

portees. Although it was not enough, this aid helped to keep them alive. By that time, international pressure and a shift in Romanian policy had led Antonescu to stop the deportations. Toward the end of 1943, when Soviet armies entered Transnistria, most survivors were allowed back into Romania. Others returned at the end of the war.

For decades, Romanian authorities denied any responsibility for what had happened in Transnistria. They argued, despite the evidence, that all atrocities had been committed by German soldiers. Since the death of President Nicolae Ceausescu in 1989, there has been a shift in that official position. Recently published government statements (1995) admit the "participation" of Romanian troops in these atrocities. Yet they insist that this was done by individuals going against explicit orders.

T R A N S Y L V A N I A

Region of central Europe which was under Hungarian rule until 1920. In that year, HUNGARY, which had sided with GERMANY during World War I, was forced to give it up to neighboring ROMANIA. When WORLD WAR II began, Hungary was once again Germany's ally. Hungary received Transylvania back under the terms of an agreement concluded with Germany and ITALY on 30 August 1940. Between 150,000 and 165,000 Jews resided in this area, mainly in the towns of Oradea, Cluj, and Satu Mare. Most of them rejoiced at being reunited with Hungary after 20 years of Romanian rule, which had been marked by antisemitism and anti-Jewish measures. Soon, however, they were subjected to growing restrictions, as were all Hungarian Jews.

No mass deportations were carried out until the occupation of Hungary by Germany in March 1944. Then, Adolf EICHMANN came to Hungary to supervise the implementation of the "FINAL SOLUTION" by confiscating Jewish property, concentrating all JEWS into GHETTOS and finally deporting them to AUSCHWITZ. A little over three months later northern Transylvania had been cleared of Jews. Most of them died in Auschwitz. Only a trickle made their way home after the war. On 20 January 1945, Romania re-annexed northern Transylvania. The 40,000 Jews of southern Transylvania, who had remained under Romanian rule, were now subjected to discriminatory measures, deprived of their property, expelled and sent away for forced labor, but no mass deportations to DEATH CAMPS were carried out.

T R A W N I K I

SS training camp and FORCED LABOR camp, located in the LUBLIN district of POLAND. Its supervisor was Odilo GLOBOCNIK.

Trawniki was established in the fall of 1941 and served two purposes. First, it trained Ukrainians, who assisted the SS in guarding GHETTOS and DEATH CAMPS and carrying out DEPORTATIONS. Second, it served as a LABOR CAMP, in which JEWS and Soviet prisoners of war worked under harsh conditions in specially established factories. Between 2,000 and 3,000 Ukrainians passed through the camp. The German guards viewed their Ukrainian assistants with contempt. Reports from Jewish survivors about the Ukrainians differ widely. Some survivors describe acts of utmost cruelty, while others mention displays of sympathy.

About 20,000 Jews passed through the camp, including many who were deported there when the WARSAW ghetto was liquidated. Many died from starvation and disease. Others were sent to their deaths at BELZEC. About 10,000 Jews were at Trawniki when, on 5 November 1943, the camp was liquidated as part of operation ERNTEFEST. In order to prevent uprisings inspired by the recent revolt at SOBIBÓR, all of the remaining Jews of Trawniki were led out of the camp and shot in ditches that had already been dug.

T R E B L I N K A

DEATH CAMP located in a sparsely populated area, along the main WARSAW–Bialystok railroad line, near Treblinka in POLAND.

A work camp was built in Treblinka in 1941. Polish and Jewish inmates worked at hard labor in the nearby quarries. The death camp was built in July 1942. It was opened by receiving the massive DEPORTATIONS of JEWS from Warsaw, which began on July 23 and continued through September. More than 265,000 Jews from Warsaw were deported the 60 miles to Treblinka.

Treblinka was a rectangle with watchtowers at each corner. The barbed wire fence surrounding

A couple of eyewitnesses escaped from Treblinka and came back to the ghetto. They told the leaders—from the Jewish Fighting Organization [ZOB] and from the Judenrat—what they saw exactly with their own eyes.... The leaders [from the ZOB] put up placards [to warn people] not to volunteer for "resettlement" because it means going to death. A lot of them didn't want to believe it.

[When the deportations started] every day a transport. They said it was eight hours one way to the Russian territories [for resettlement] and eight hours [for the train] back. But the trains went and returned in four hours. They only went about 50 miles. The railroad workers who were in the Polish underground, who helped the Jewish underground in the ghetto, investigated. Some of these people made marks on the outside of the trains [before they left] so they knew they were the same trains. They knew they were coming back too soon. They wanted to investigate it, to see how long it took. They were railroad workers. They knew the timing and the distances. These workers took the trains to a main railroad place about 20 miles from [Treblinka]. [The Nazis] changed the engineers to all Germans and the trains went onto a different siding with a small engine. This was on a dirt road concealed by the forest. The Polish railroad workers were suspicious and found out from the local population who saw this and were suspicious too. They couldn't figure out where they were going, and [why they] were empty coming back. What are they doing with the people?

From the testimony of Jack Price, Gratz College Oral History Archives

the camp was hidden by woods. Some 20 to 30 Germans, mainly veterans of the so-called "EUTHANASIA PROGRAM," were assisted by 90 to 120 Ukrainians and others in staffing the camp. They were supplemented by Jewish prisoners forced into the work.

Imfried Eberl was the first commandant of the camp. He was replaced by Franz STANGL in the spring of 1942.

Jews were deported from GHETTOS by train. A special railroad track led directly into the camp. The Jews were forced off the train and sent into two barracks, men on one side, women and CHILDREN on the other. There they were forced to undress and leave their valuables. Women's hair was shaved and all prisoners were forced up a path, known as the pipe, into the GAS CHAMBERS. Poison carbon monoxide gas was sent through pipes that appeared as shower heads. This fooled some prisoners who thought they were being sent to showers. Those who could not walk—the elderly or the ill—were sent to the "infirmary," and shot on the spot. Meanwhile, prisoners' clothing was sorted, identifying marks were removed, and the railroad cars were cleaned and prepared for their next mission. Gold teeth were removed from the dead before their bodies were burned in large open trenches.

The pace of killing was so rapid that the three original gas chambers were increased to ten between August and October 1942.

Between 750,000 and 870,000 Jews from Warsaw, Radom, LUBLIN, BIALYSTOK, SLOVAKIA, THERESIENSTADT, GREECE, and MACEDONIA were killed there along with 2,000 GYPSIES. The camp was ordered closed by SS chief Heinrich HIMMLER in the summer of 1943. As in the other AKTION REINHARD camps, the bodies were dug up and burned. Bone crushers were used to destroy evidence of the crime.

An armed revolt broke out on 2 August 1943, as Treblinka was about to be taken apart. Jews took weapons from the armory, fired on the guards, and burned buildings. Some 70 inmates were able to escape.

There were three trials of Treblinka guards, two in Dusseldorf, GERMANY, and one in Jerusalem, ISRAEL. Between October 1964 and August 1965, 10 defendants were put on trial. Four were sentenced to life imprisonment, five were sentenced to three to twelve years of prison and one was acquitted. Franz Stangl, the camp commandant, who had escaped to Brazil after the war, was tried in 1970. He was sentenced to life imprisonment.

The Israeli government tried John Demjanuk, a Ukrainian who had been brought from the United

Camp model of Treblinka Camp, Ghetto Fighters' Museum, Israel

States. He was found guilty by the court of being "Ivan the Terrible," a particularly sadistic guard at Treblinka. When the case was appealed, Demjanuk was acquitted by the Israeli Supreme Court because of doubts about his identification, even though he had clearly served as a guard in another death camp—SOBIBÓR.

The Polish government has erected a monument of great beauty and simplicity on the site of the Treblinka death camp. It includes thousands of stone sculptures outlining the camp, the railroad tracks and the pipe. On them are inscribed the names of the destroyed Jewish communities of Poland. It has become a site of constant pilgrimage.

TREPPER, LEOPOLD

see RED ORCHESTRA.

TRIALS OF WAR CRIMINALS

The prosecution of political and military leaders of the Nazi Reich for war crimes. Three categories of crime were defined before the first NUREMBERG TRIAL: crimes against peace, war crimes, and CRIMES AGAINST HUMANITY. Even before the war ended, a number of

trials had taken place—in Krasnodov, Russia in June 1943, of Soviet citizens who had participated in mass killings; in Kharkóv, Russia where the defendants were also killers; and in MAJDANEK immediately following its liberation. In later trials, others besides the actual killers were also among the accused. These included the organizers, policy makers, and others who contributed to committing these crimes—including the judges of the Nazi legal system. The International Military Tribunal at Nuremberg judged the highest Nazi leaders in its main case.

Early in the war, there were warnings that the Nazi leaders would be held accountable for crimes against civilians. In 1940, joint statements issued by GREAT BRITAIN, POLAND, CZECHOSLOVAKIA, and FRANCE held the Nazi regime responsible for criminal acts. In 1941, Winston CHURCHILL stated, "retribution for these crimes must take its place among the major purposes of the war." The following October, with the United States now involved in the fighting, President Franklin D. ROOSEVELT stated, "just and sure punishment must be meted out to the ringleaders." By 26 October 1943, the UNITED NATIONS WAR CRIMES COMMISSION was formed by 15 Allied nations. It established at that time, that the responsible leaders would be the principal target for post-war justice.

Trial in Frankfurt of 22 Germans accused of crimes in Auschwitz

After the war, the Allied victors put considerable effort into determining what method they would use to bring the Nazis to justice at Nuremberg and following trials. There was some resistance to the idea of a trial at all, both by the Soviets and the British. Many believed it was a foregone conclusion that the leaders would be executed. Thus some in Great Britain favored summary execution by military tribunal. American Supreme Court Justice Robert Jackson, who was later appointed by President Harry S. TRUMAN to prosecute at Nuremberg, summed up the dangers of trial: "The ultimate principle is that you must put no man on trial if you are not willing to see him freed if not proved guilty." In other words, by committing themselves to try major Nazi war criminals publicly in courts of International Law, the Allies ran the risk of not being able to earn convictions.

Three reasons led to the decision to prosecute the criminals according to International Law. First, there was a strong preference on the part of the Americans for authentic justice over punishment and revenge. Second, the Nazis had left a "paper trail" which made it possible to tell the story of German atrocities accurately. The mountain of documents recovered following the war revealed the true organization of Nazi GERMANY. Scores of researchers for the prosecution worked through these papers to build the case. The Allies had the capacity to prove that the war crimes originated from the highest levels of government and filtered down to those who committed them. Third, the case against the leaders had to be proven to the German people. U.S. Secretary of State Cordell Hull argued that justice, based on documentation and testimony, would "meet the judgment of history so that the Germans will not be able to claim that an admission of war guilt was exacted from them under duress."

After the first Nuremberg Trial, there were 12 other trials, each focusing on a different aspect of the atrocities. These included the "Medical Case" against Nazi doctors (see MEDICAL EXPERIMENTS), and the case against the EINSATZGRUPPEN. In these trials, 177 Nazi criminals were convicted, and 12 death sentences were imposed. These trials ended in 1949.

Several other important trials took place in the Allied Occupation Zone following the war. From 17 September to 17 November 1945, the British military tribunal tried the SS guards of the BERGEN-BELSEN and AUSCHWITZ concentration camps. In March 1946, a British tribunal in Hamburg tried the manufacturers of ZYKLON B or prussic acid. These were the chemical crystals used in the gas chambers at Auschwitz. The Tesch and Stabenow Company of Hamburg had been supplying Auschwitz from 1941 with the chemical which was originally used as a disinfectant. The defense argued that they did not know what their product was used for. However, the prosecution successfully proved that Bruno Tesch visited the camp itself and therefore knew of the intended use of his product. In the end, its directors, Tesch and Karl Weinbacher were sentenced to death and executed. This established an important legal principle: manufacturing gas for killing prisoners is a war crime. In the I.G. FARBEN Case, which involved charges against the directors of that company for selling Zyklon B and other charges, the defendants were found guilty of crimes against humanity but by 1951 all had been freed.

According to the Moscow Declaration of 1943, the Allied powers had agreed that accused war criminals would be sent for trial to the country in which the crimes were committed. Therefore, the major Auschwitz criminals were tried in WARSAW, beginning on 2 April 1947. Between this trial and those following, there were a total of 617 defendants, with 34 death sentences delivered. Among those executed were Rudolf HÖSS, the first commandant of the camp, his successor Arthur Liebehenschel, and 23 SS members. From 1958, German courts began their own legal investigations into the crimes of Auschwitz. In 1965, there were another six convictions. In Austria, additional prosecutions of SS men from Auschwitz were undertaken. The camp doctor, Horst Fischer was convicted and executed. While there appears to have been a relatively large number of prosecutions among the Auschwitz staff, the figure seems less impressive when it is remembered that the total number of SS staff was more than 6,000.

By 1949, the Allied prosecutors had fully uncovered the role of the main branches of the German government in the murder of the JEWS. In essence, the world had been exposed to a new type of criminal: the bureaucratic killer. The International Tribunals then turned to prosecuting individuals who played roles in the Holocaust. However, at the same time, the courts now entered into a race with the statutes of limitations, the legal time limit after which various crimes could not be prosecuted. By May 1960, the statute of limitations had expired on all war-related crimes except murder.

After 1960, several other war criminals were brought to trial. The most significant was Adolf EICHMANN, tried in Israel in 1961, and the trial of Klaus BARBIE in France in 1988. Into the 1990s, aging Nazis were still being located—often in Latin America—and brought to trial. According to the registry of the Central Office for the Investigation of Nazi Crimes in Ludwigsburg, West Germany, over 90,000 persons had been investigated in West German courts alone for participating in Nazi crimes by 1986. However in 1955, a mere decade after the HOLOCAUST, less than 400 Nazis war criminals were still in German jails. A further 13,000 were convicted in East Germany up to 1976. Other countries have also brought large numbers to trial—40,000 in Hungary, 15,000 in the Netherlands, 5,500 in Poland—to name only a few. The U.S. Department of Justice in 1979 established an Office of Special Investigation to track down Nazi war criminals who had found refuge in the United States. Some of these were extradited to stand trial in the countries where the crimes had been committed. However, the passage of time means the ending of war crimes trials. The defendants are aged. Cases are harder to build, since evidence from over 50 years ago is hard to collect. This is especially true of the testimony of living witnesses, whose memories cannot always be relied upon after the long lapse of time. Over the

Hans Morgenthau, (1908-1980) was a Jewish lawyer and academic who fled Nazi Germany. While teaching political science at the University of Chicago following the war, Morgenthau had this interchange with a student who happened to be a former captain in Rommel's Afrika Korps. The student asked Morgenthau "How can you speak of your fine ideals and Western morality when you look at what the Allies have done to Germany? Do you call that justice?" Morgenthau replied: "No, I do not call that justice. If the Allies had done justice, they would have treated Germany as Rome treated Carthage. They would have killed every man, woman and child, and they would have salted the earth so that nothing would grow there again. That would have been justice." Morgenthau then strode out of the room, leaving the captain speechless.

(From *Remembering Hans Morgenthau*, David Fromkin)

past 50 years, many of the Nazis and their collaborators have been brought to trial—but there can be no doubt that many more have escaped justice.

TRUMAN, HARRY S.

(1884–1972) Thirty-third president of the United States (1945–1953). Truman, a former judge and senator, was chosen by the Democratic Party to be, President Franklin D. ROOSEVELT'S vice-presidential running mate, in 1944. He then became president when Roosevelt died on 12 April 1945, less than a month before the Germans surrendered. As early as 1943, Senator Truman (Missouri) had taken a strong stand in support of European Jewry. He stated to an audience of 25,000 in Chicago that "This is not a Jewish problem, it is an American problem and we must and we will face it squarely and honorably."

As president of the United States, he was openly in favor of helping Jewish CAMP survivors and homeless REFUGEES. In July 1945, he acted to remove measures that discriminated against JEWS in the DISPLACED PERSONS Act. In 1946, he issued a strong call for 100,000 DISPLACED PERSONS to be admitted to PALESTINE,

but this was not accepted by the British government. He was convinced that Palestine was the only satisfactory answer to the question of the resettlement of Jewish refugees. This led him to support the establishment of a Jewish state in Palestine, in spite of the opposition of many members of his administration. Truman resisted the two most commonly used arguments against the creation of a Jewish state: it would antagonize the oil lobby and the Arab states; and the United States would have to send troops to defend it. He insisted that the settlement of the refugees was a basic human problem that had to be solved. He decided to have the United States vote for the Partition Plan at the United Nations on 29 November 1947. In May 1948, his government was the first to recognize the newly proclaimed State of ISRAEL.

TUNISIA

Country in northern Africa. In the summer of 1940, FRANCE was divided between the Nazi conquerors in the north and the pro-Nazi VICHY government in the south. Most of the French administration in Tunisia declared loyalty to Vichy. On 30 November 1940,

Italian Prisoners of War in Tunisia, 1943

British artillery at Abu-Arada, Tunisia

racial laws were introduced. As a result, all JEWS employed in government jobs were fired, and all Jewish students in state-owned schools were forced to leave. Late in 1942, a quarter of a million German and Italian soldiers withdrawing from other North African countries joined the pro-Vichy French troops in Tunisia. On 14 November, the capital city, Tunis, was taken over by the Germans. For almost six months, Tunisia was directly ruled by the Nazis. The new governor was General Walter Nehring. He was assisted by SS Officer Walther Rauff, who had been in charge of killing almost 200,000 Jews and others in western Russia. Rauff headed the SS in Tunisia between July 1942 and May 1943. The SS closed down the offices of the Jewish community in Tunis and arrested all the leaders. The community had to pay an enormous ransom for their release. The same sum was demanded of the community in Sfax, under the threat that 30 of their leaders would be executed if the ransom were not paid.

The Nazis ordered Jews throughout Tunisia to bring all kinds of property to the offices of the government. Some Jewish women were raped and some Jewish men and women were shot and killed. In certain places, the Jews were required to wear yellows stars, inscribed with the word *"Juif"*— French for "Jew." The main synagogue of Tunis was turned into a warehouse. Four thousand Jewish men were arrested as hostages in case of revolt, and sent to 32 FORCED LABOR CAMPS. The largest and harshest of these was Bizerte. Conditions in the camps were inhuman. The main type of labor carried out by these prisoners was the building of barricades and military airports, the transportation of ammunition, and road repair. Some of the prisoners were killed during this time. In February 1943, the SS deported 11 prominent Jews to CONCENTRATION and DEATH CAMPS in Europe. This was meant as the first step in the Nazis' plan to destroy the entire Jewish community.

However, before that plan could be carried out, the British army entered Tunis on 7 May. It is estimated that a few hundred Tunisian Jews were killed by the Nazis. The exact number is unknown.

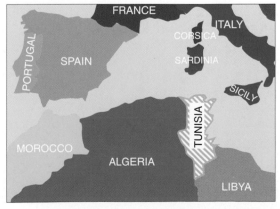

𝒰

U K R A I N E

Former Soviet Russian republic (today an independent state) in east-central Europe. In 1939, there were about 1.75 million JEWS in the country.

When the Soviets occupied eastern Poland (to which many Jews from German-occupied POLAND had fled) and annexed northern BUKOVINA in 1940, the Jewish population of Ukraine increased dramatically. On the eve of the German invasion there were 2.5 million Jews in Ukraine.

The fate of the Ukrainian Jews was different in each of the three major parts of the territory. The Jews of western Ukraine (eastern Galicia and Volhynia) fell under the GENERALGOUVERNEMENT. As such, many were closed in GHETTOS and shared the fate of the rest of Polish Jewry. A large number were deported to DEATH CAMPS, mostly to BELZEC. Others were killed in or near their homes.

The fate of the Jews of northern Bukovina was partly decided by the Romanian authorities. Many of the Jews in that area were deported to TRANSNISTRIA, and about 50 percent of them survived.

The Ukrainian interior (the prewar territory of the country) was where the EINSATZGRUPPEN operated. These mobile killing units were responsible for the deaths of hundreds of thousands of Jews, mostly in local massacres. The largest was carried out at BABI YAR outside KIEV in September 1941. There, 33,771 Jews were gunned down in two days.

Parade of Ukrainian volunteers to fight alongside the German army in Russia before leaving for the front. Stanislavov, Ukraine, July 1943

There was a long tradition of popular ANTISEMITISM in Ukraine. This was strengthened by Ukrainian hatred for the Soviet government, which in Ukrainian eyes was supported by Jews. Thus, the Ukrainian population saw the German occupation as an opportunity to settle scores with the Jews. It was also an opportunity for wholesale looting. The Ukrainian nationalist leadership expected that SOVIET RUSSIA would be defeated and that the Germans would then establish an independent Ukraine in the region under German influence.

Particularly in western Ukraine, where Ukrainian nationalism was most widespread, Ukrainians robbed and murdered their Jewish neighbors with an eagerness and brutality that shocked even the Germans. The Germans were quick to take advantage of Ukrainian antisemitism. They encouraged savage pogroms in many cities and towns, and thousands of Jews lost their lives. The worst of these took place in LVOV. The Ukrainians collaborated enthusiastically with the Germans. Two Ukrainian intelligence units were attached to the German army, and Ukrainian police and local authorities were set up by the German military government.

Ukrainians were recruited in large numbers to participate in massacres. It was left to Ukrainian administrators and guards to determine conditions within ghettos. This power was usually used to force Jews to hand over their property and then to kill them. At the same time, a small number of Ukrainians risked their own lives to save Jews.

UMSCHLAGPLATZ

("Transfer Point")

The DEPORTATION point for JEWS from WARSAW, who were sent to the TREBLINKA DEATH CAMP some 60 miles away.

During the summer of 1942, more than 265,000 Jews were rounded up in the GHETTO, marched to the Umschlagplatz and transported in cattle cars to their deaths.

The most famous march to the Umschlagplatz occurred on 6 August 1942, when the Nazis raided the children's institutions in the Warsaw ghetto. Janusz KORCZAK, a well-known Polish Jewish educator and teacher, was head of the children's orphanage. He knew that his CHILDREN would be sent to their deaths

Jews gathered for deportation in the Warsaw Umschlagplatz

at Treblinka. He lined the children up in groups of four. The orphans were clutching flasks of water and their favorite books and toys. There were 192 children and 10 adults. They marched through the ghetto to the Umschlagplatz, where they joined thousands of people waiting in the boiling August sun. There was no shade, shelter, water, or bathrooms at the deportation point. Yet the children did not cry and scream as people usually did when forced to board the trains. They walked quietly in rows of four. They had been calmed by Korczak, who refused to leave them, even at the time of death. In 1988, a monument was dedicated at the site.

U N D E R G R O U N D

Many activities that had been forbidden by the Nazis were carried out secretly in underground situations. Underground movements developed especially in GHETTOS. They took many forms. Some were designed to help the JEWS with physical and spiritual support. Others worked to fight the Nazis and smuggle Jews out of the ghettos.

Often, there were many small underground groups and one coordinating body. The activities performed by the underground included education, social welfare, religious observance and study, cultural work, and upkeep of orphanages and old people's homes. These activities lifted the morale of the Jews and created a sense of self-esteem and group solidarity (see SELF-HELP). Political undergrounds planned armed defiance and spread information (see RESISTANCE).

The ghetto undergrounds circulated many underground newspapers with news of the war and other developments. These were secret: the reader knew only the person from whom he or she received the paper and the person to whom it was then passed. Reports were gathered from illegal homemade radios that picked up the British and Russian broadcasting stations. The papers not only gave the news but included items intended to lift the spirits of the reader.

An important function of the underground was to establish contacts and coordinate among the different ghettos and the various resistance movements. Many of those who undertook these difficult tasks were young women, who could travel around with

Underground military group in Belgium

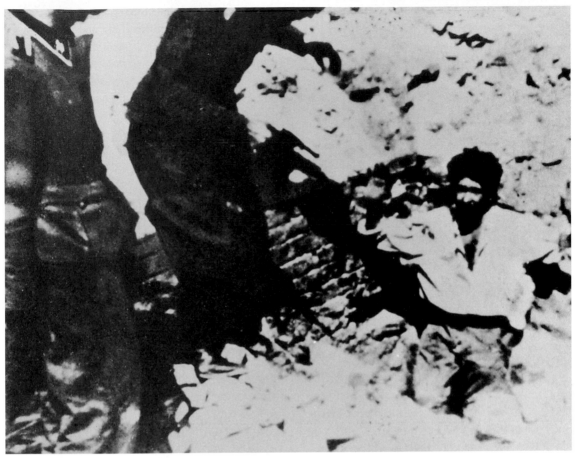

Underground activist caught in Warsaw

less risk than the men. These messengers were among the heroines of the Holocaust, as their lives were always in danger.

UNION GÉNÉRALE DES ISRAÉLITES DE FRANCE

(UGIF; "General Union of French Jews")

Organization set up by VICHY's commissioner-general for Jewish affairs, Xavier VALLAT, to bring together all the Jewish organizations of FRANCE into a single Jewish council.

The UGIF was set up by the Vichy government in November 1941, in response to German demands. Two councils were set up, one in the occupied zone of France, and one in the unoccupied zone (Vichy).

Vallat assured Jewish leaders that the role of the UGIF would be to provide social aid to Jews. However, its main purpose was to allow the Germans easier access to the large amount of funds held by the different Jewish organizations in France.

The UGIF performed a similar function to that of the JUDENRAT (Jewish Councils) of eastern Europe. In May 1943, the Germans threatened to arrest the heads of the UGIF unless they were given names of all Jewish RESISTANCE workers.

In 1944, the new secretary-general for Jewish affairs, Joseph Antignac, denounced the heads of the UGIF in both the northern and southern parts of France. Vallat and Antignac were deported to AUSCHWITZ.

One of the last actions of the Germans in France was to deport to their deaths 300 CHILDREN from UGIF orphanages in the vicinity of PARIS.

UNITED FIGHTERS ORGANIZATION

SEE FAREYNEGTE PARTIZANER ORGANIZATSYE (FPO).

UNITED NATIONS RELIEF AND REHABILITATION ADMINISTRATION (UNRRA)

Organization created by the Allies in 1943 to aid people who were displaced by WORLD WAR II (see DISPLACED PERSONS). Teams of UNRRA workers followed the military forces into Europe after the liberation. They had to decide which of the millions of REFUGEES were officially displaced persons (DPs) and arrange for their return home. Meanwhile, the UNRRA looked after the physical, psychological, and employment needs of the DPs in special camps. By the end of June 1945, there were 322 teams helping to run transit centers and DP camps. They had many problems to deal with: severe food and clothing shortages, language problems, the threat of epidemics, the huge task of reuniting families, and aiding the thousands of unaccompanied CHILDREN in their care. In the years after the war, the original DPs in Central Europe were joined in the UNRRA camps by an influx of survivors from Eastern Europe, most of them Jews.

The Allies had thought that all DPs would want to return home. However, this proved not to be the case, particularly for the Jewish DPs. They did not want to return to their former towns where whole communities had been wiped out and no homes remained. They preferred to stay in the DP camps and wait for a visa to America, PALESTINE or another country.

UNRRA's role in 1947—when 640,000 DPs were still in its charge—was eventually taken over by the Preparatory Commission for the International Refugee Organization. The UNRRA had also helped DPs in many countries outside Europe, including Egypt and China.

UNITED NATIONS WAR CRIMES COMMISSION

(UNWCC)

International body created in October 1943 to prosecute war criminals. It was made up of representatives of 15 Allied nations. After a dispute with the other Allies, SOVIET RUSSIA did not participate.

As early as 1939, reports of Nazi crimes became known. Winston CHURCHILL, Franklin D. ROOSEVELT and Vyacheslav Molotov (Soviet foreign minister) had warned the Nazi leadership that the Allies planned to hold them accountable for war crimes. On 1 November 1943, "major criminals" were defined in a Soviet statement as those whose "offenses have no

Staff and children of the Zeilsheim Center for Child Survivors run by UNRRA

particular geographical location and who will be punished by a joint decision of the governments of the Allies."

The UNWCC began by deciding on the legal categories for the various types of CRIMES AGAINST HUMANITY. It conducted investigations and prepared indictments (official accusations) of individuals. Following the war, it helped establish the major registries (official lists) of war criminals. It organized the evidence found in Nazi archives. It set up the courts to try the criminals and also helped in capturing them. By the time it had completed its work, the UNWCC had collected files on over 36,000 suspects. It had gathered important source material on all aspects of the HOLOCAUST.

The UNWCC was disbanded in February 1948. Not all countries agreed to follow UNWCC guidelines and turn over Nazis who had taken refuge with them. The Soviets insisted on punishing war criminals by themselves. These decisions restricted the UNWCC's achievements.

UNITED STATES AND THE HOLOCAUST

Between 1933 and 1941, the goal of Nazi anti-Jewish policy was to make GERMANY and the lands it occupied "*Judenrein*" (free of Jews), through forced emigration. The Jews of Europe looked desperately for places of refuge. First and foremost, they thought of the United States with its long, great history as a land of refuge. However, since the 1920s, a strict quota system limited the entry of immigrants to the United States according to their country of origin. A potential immigrant had to find financial guarantees that he would not become a charge on the State. American Consular officials erected "paper walls" to restrict immigration. Only once during the 12 years of Nazi rule was the quota for Germany and AUSTRIA filled.

President Franklin D. ROOSEVELT made some gestures from which little emerged. He convened—but did not attend—an unsuccessful conference at Evian (see EVIAN CONFERENCE) in 1938 to deal with the international REFUGEE crisis.

The president was hampered by considerations at home. Slowly recovering from economic depression, one-third of all Americans were ill clothed, ill housed, and ill fed. Many voices in the country demanded isolation, stressing that America came first. The president, who was trying to overcome American isolationism, was hesitant to lose potential support by focusing on European JEWS.

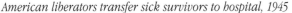

American liberators transfer sick survivors to hospital, 1945

His stand was supported by the public. Even American Jews were hesitant to pressure for a more benevolent refugee policy (see AMERICAN JEWRY AND THE HOLOCAUST).

Efforts to rescue CHILDREN too young to work were not successful (see RESCUE OF CHILDREN). The 1939 Wagner-Rogers Bill to admit 20,000 German children under the age of 14 never received consideration in the floor of Congress. While there was still time to save the Jews, no country offered refuge.

Once the United States entered WORLD WAR II on 8 December 1941, absolute priority was given to winning the war. The refugee problem would have to wait until the war ended.

The United States had early and reliable information about the plan to annihilate the Jews of Europe. On 11 August 1942, Dr. Gerhart Riegner, the WORLD JEWISH CONGRESS representative in SWITZERLAND, sent a secret cable through secure channels to the State Department to pass on to the American Jewish leader, Rabbi Stephen S. WISE. The cable told Wise of the Nazi plans to exterminate the Jews (see RIEGNER CABLE).

The State Department did not pass the cable on to Rabbi Wise until he approached them. He was then asked not to make the information public until it could be confirmed by additional sources. Confirmation received was forthcoming in the fall and early winter of 1942, when the GHETTOS of POLAND were being emptied and the DEATH CAMPS were in full operation.

In early 1943, the State Department tried to shut

American troops from the 183rd Engineer Combat Battalion of the 8th Corps, U.S. Third Army, are shown a stack of corpses lying outside the crematorium.

U.S. Army units at the liberaton of Paris, 1944

down the channel through which it would have received information about the Jews. It did not want domestic political considerations to interfere with the conduct of the war.

News of the "FINAL SOLUTION" came from other sources as well, such as the mission of Jan KARSKI, a secret courier for the Polish GOVERNMENT-IN-EXILE. Karski met with top American and British officials, including President Roosevelt, and informed them of the existence of CONCENTRATION CAMPS and death camps.

Bowing to domestic pressures, another fruitless refugee conference was convened in Bermuda in April 1943 by GREAT BRITAIN and the United States to give the impression that something was being done (see BERMUDA CONFERENCE).

The harshest judgment of the American policy toward the Holocaust was detailed in a 13 January 1944 staff memo given to Secretary of Treasury Henry MORGENTHAU, Jr., entitled "Report to the Secretary of the Acquiescence of This Government in the Murder of the Jews" (see box).

On 16 January 1944, Morgenthau went to the White House to see Roosevelt and handed him a condensed version of the report he had received. Morgenthau presented a proposal for actively involving the United States in the business

"Report to the Secretary of the Acquiescence of This Government in the Murder of the Jews," handed to Henry J. Morgenthau Jr. by members of the treasury

The memo charged that State Department officials had used governmental machinery to prevent the rescue of these Jews. Had taken steps designed to prevent the rescue programs of private organizations from being put into effect. And that in their official capacity they had gone so far as to secretly attempt to stop the obtaining of information concerning the murder of the Jewish population of Europe. They had tried to cover up their guilt by: a) concealment and misrepresentation; b) giving false and misleading explanations for their failures to act and their attempts to prevent action; and c) issuing false and misleading statements concerning the "action" which they had taken to date.

of rescue. Within days of the meeting, President Roosevelt established the WAR REFUGEE BOARD (WRB).

The WRB tried to get Roosevelt to publish statements condemning the murder of Jews, and to draw up plans for postwar TRIALS OF WAR CRIMINALS. It also argued for the bombing of AUSCHWITZ (see AUSCHWITZ BOMBING). Its requests were denied. However, it did carry out on a number of successful rescue attempts.

Until 1944, American policy toward the Jews was influenced by ANTISEMITISM within the State Department, domestic politics, and the relative powerlessness and disunity of American Jews. The United States did not formally sponsor rescue efforts until the seventh year of Nazi rule.

After the war, American soldiers in Europe discovered first-hand the horrors of the Holocaust and the problem of the refugees (see DISPLACED PERSONS). Only then did the United States become more active in helping the Jewish survivors. President Harry S. TRUMAN was personally moved by their plight and became involved in efforts to find a solution. This eventually led to enlarging immigrant quotas in the United States and America's speedy recognition of the newly-founded State of ISRAEL IN 1948.

UNITED STATES HOLOCAUST MEMORIAL MUSEUM

Museum dedicated to the memory of the millions of men, women and children who were victims of the HOLOCAUST. The Museum also stands as a reminder of the responsibility of all individuals in a

The National Holocaust Museum, Washington, D.C.

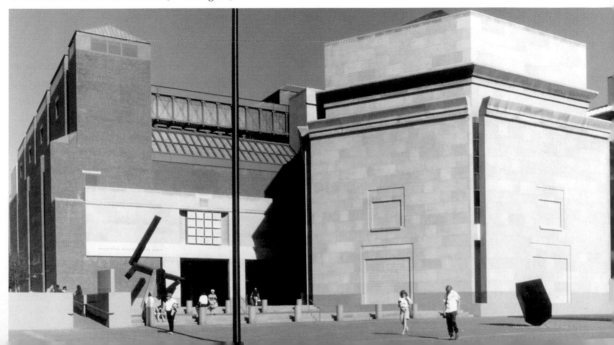

Inside the National Holocaust Museum, 1000 Raoul Wallenberg Place SW (15th Street at Independence Avenue), Washington, D.C., 20024-2150. Telephone: (202) 488-0400. Open daily from 10:00 A.M. to 5:30 P.M. Timed tickets are required for admission to the permanent exhibition which is not recommended for children under 12 years of age. Free tickets for admission on the same day are available at the box office beginning at 9:00 A.M. and they are often gone by noon. Tickets are available in advance for a fee; call (202) 432-7328 or 1-800-571-7328. Groups of 10 or more must schedule four weeks ahead. Tickets are not needed for the Hall of Remembrance, the Learning Center and special exhibits. There is an extensive research library, a resource center, a shop and a cafeteria. The museum is accessible to persons with disabilities. Elevators serve all areas.

free society to protect human freedom.

In 1978, President Jimmy Carter appointed a President's Commission on the Holocaust, headed by author Elie WIESEL. In 1980, the United States Holo-

caust Memorial Council was established by a unanimous act of Congress. Harvey A. Meyerhoff, a philanthropist and real estate developer, was appointed in 1987 by President Ronald Reagan to succeed Wiesel. This council was asked to plan and build a national institution dedicated to remembering and teaching about the Holocaust. In 1989, Jeshajahu Weinberg, who had created the Museum of the Diaspora in Israel, was appointed museum director.

The museum, opened in 1993, is located 1,500 feet from the Washington Monument, next to the Mall in Washington D.C. It is built on public lands with funds donated by the American people. The museum was designed by the architect James Ingo Freed. He visited a number of Holocaust sites, including ghettos and camps, so that the museum would capture the feeling and the spirit of the historical event. Raw brick, exposed metal beams and rivets, boarded windows, steel gates, fences and barriers all combine to give the visitor an eerie feeling. The overall effect, Freed says, "tells the visitor something is amiss here."

Unlike most other similar institutions, the museum not only displays artifacts, photographs and maps; it also attempts to use the exhibits as educational tools. The permanent exhibition, the special exhibitions, and the Wexner Learning Center are educational in nature. The Holocaust Research Institute, a center for scholarship and research, contains an extensive library, vast photo and film archives, and a collection of testimony by Holocaust survivors, perpetrators, and liberators. The Learning Center serves students and teachers. It contains an interactive, computer-based facility where visitors may access texts, film footage, movies and music.

The archives house a registry which contains the names, cities of birth, camps of incarceration, places of liberation and communities of resettlement for more than 70,000 survivors who came to the United States in the aftermath of the Holocaust.

Holocaust scholar Michael Berenbaum notes that, "on entering the museum, visitors can punch into a computer and receive an identity card—for an actual person of the same gender, who was their age at the time of the Holocaust. As visitors move through the exhibition, they can find out what was happening at a given historical moment to their historical 'twin'. Visitors learn, before they leave the exhibition, whether that person survived or perished. The personalization of the experience brings the visitor face to face with history."

There is a self-guided tour of one hour, recommended for visitors 11 years of age or older, which focuses on the theme of Rescue and Resistance. It directs visitors to exhibits on the rescue efforts of communities such as LE CHAMBON SUR LIGNON; the responses of nations (BULGARIA, DENMARK, ITALY and the WAR REFUGEE BOARD); the initiatives of individuals (RAOUL WALLENBERG), and Jewish RESISTANCE.

USSR (UNION OF SOVIET SOCIALIST REPUBLICS)

see SOVIET RUSSIA.

U S T A S H A

Croatian fascist nationalist movement (see FASCISM AND FASCIST MOVEMENTS) founded in 1929 by Ante PAVELIC.

After World War I, CROATIA was incorporated as part of YUGOSLAVIA. The Ustasha (meaning "rebel")

had a number of central beliefs: fierce nationalism, extremely conservative Catholicism, antisemitism, and anti-communism. It opposed the Yugoslav Kingdom of Serbs and Croats, which was dominated by the Serb royal family. Pavelic was a plotter of the 1934 murder of King Alexander of Yugoslavia.

The Nazi conquest of YUGOSLAVIA in 1941 gave the Ustasha its opportunity to form the "independent" Croatian state that it wanted. Pavelic became the head of state—and dictator—of the fascist Croatian regime.

The Ustasha-led government was extremely barbaric. Those whom the movement saw as its enemies—Serbs, Jews and leftists—suffered horribly at the hands of Pavelic and his followers. At the JASENOVAC CONCENTRATION CAMP, which was established by the Ustasha, torture was common and often involved axes and knives. Over 800,000 enemies of the regime were murdered by the Ustasha in Jasenovac alone.

The Ustasha-led state came to an end in May 1945. Pavelic took refuge in Argentina and is still regarded by some Croatians as a patriotic hero.

Ustasha soldiers confiscating Jewish property in Croatia

V

VA'AD HA-HATSALA

(Rescue Committee)

Rescue committee of the Union of Orthodox Rabbis of the United States and Canada, the central organization of American Orthodox rabbis. Thousands of European Jews were saved from the Nazis by the Va'ad. Its leader was Eliezer Silver of Cincinnati.

When WORLD WAR II broke out, the committee was interested in sending relief and rescuing the approximately 2,500 rabbis and yeshiva (rabbinical academy) students who had escaped from German-occupied Poland to LITHUANIA (which was under Soviet rule until 1941). It helped 650 rabbis and yeshiva students to leave Lithuania by 1941. About 150 went to the United States, and 500 were able to obtain visas to SHANGHAI.

After the Japanese went to war with the United States in December 1941, the rabbis and rabbinical students in Shanghai were placed in a difficult position. Thus, the activities of the va'ad focused on aiding them, as well as several hundred yeshiva students in Soviet Central Asia. The aid provided by the committee allowed these groups to maintain their religious life-style and study routines under difficult conditions.

In 1942, news of Adolf HITLER's plan to murder the JEWS of Europe became known. At the beginning of September 1942, the committee representative in SWITZERLAND, Isaac Sternbuch, sent a telegram to New York with news of the mass murder of Jews in eastern Europe and specifically in the WARSAW ghetto. The committee shifted its activities to the rescue of Jews in eastern Europe.

In contrast to most other American Jewish organizations, the committee tried to pressure the American government to act (see AMERICAN JEWRY AND THE HOLOCAUST). On 6 October 1943, 400 Orthodox rabbis marched on Washington to protest America's inaction. This was the only mass demonstration of a Jewish group in Washington during the war. The attention drawn by this march contributed to the founding in January 1944 of the WAR REFUGEE BOARD—the only official United States government organization devoted to rescue.

By 1944, the extent of the destruction process was known to the leaders of the Va'ad. They decided to concentrate on rescuing any Jew still alive in Europe—whether a yeshiva student or not. The Va'ad maintained offices in neutral countries—Switzerland, SWEDEN, Turkey—which aided in the rescue of Jews.

In order to rescue Jews, the committee was prepared to act as mediator between opposing sides. Its most successful negotiation was between SS chief Heinrich HIMMLER and a Swiss politician. It resulted in the rescue to Switzerland in February 1945 of 1,200 prisoners from the THERESIENSTADT ghetto.

After the war, the Va'ad aided Holocaust SURVIVORS.

VA'ADAT HA-EZRA VE-HA-HATZALA BE-BUDAPEST

see RELIEF AND RESCUE COMMITTEE OF BUDAPEST.

VALLAT, XAVIER

(1891–1972) The first commissioner-general for Jewish Affairs in FRANCE's VICHY government. He lost an eye and a leg fighting in the French army in World War I.

Vallat was first elected to the French parliament in 1919, as a right-wing nationalist. He made frequent attacks on JEWS in parliament. In 1940, Marshal PÉTAIN made him responsible for veterans' affairs in his government. In 1941, Vallat was appointed first commissioner-general for Jewish Affairs. He worked for the DEPORTATION of non-French Jews from Vichy and introduced antisemitic laws.

In late 1941, Vallat set up the UNION GÉNÉRALE DES IS-RAÉLITES DE FRANCE, the council of Jewish communities in France. This organization did much of the administrative work for the Nazis, including gathering names and addresses of Jews throughout France. However, Vallat did not accept some of the most extreme German anti-Jewish policies. For this he was dismissed from office because of German pressure in March 1942. Louis DARQUIER DE PELLEPOIX was appointed his successor. In 1947, Vallat was sentenced to ten years in prison, but was released two years later.

V A T I C A N

see CHRISTIAN CHURCHES; PIUS XII.

V I C H Y

Spa town in central FRANCE; seat of the wartime government that collaborated with the Germans. Fol-lowing the invasion of northern France, including PARIS, by German forces in May 1940, the French National Assembly gave full powers to Marshal Philippe PÉTAIN to negotiate an armistice settlement with the Nazis. Pétain moved to Vichy in June 1940 and formed a government led by Pierre LAVAL which collaborated with the German authorities in the northern zone of France while retaining sovereignty over the southern zone. Vichy played a key part in the establishment and implementation of antisemitic legislation and in the deportation of JEWS from France. In October 1940, entirely without pressure from the Germans, the Vichy government issued the *Statut des Juifs*, which designated an inferior status in French law to Jews. It required every Jew in France to register with the police, and established a quota limiting the number of Jews allowed to enter particular professions and public places. French internment and CONCENTRATION CAMPS, such as the camp at DRANCY, were set up and almost exclusively run by the French. Between 1940 and 1944,

A poster of Marshal Pétain calling on the French people to trust him

Vichy organized roundups of Jews in both zones. Seventy-five thousand Jews were deported to the east from France, of whom around 2,000 survived.

For many years after the war, the Vichy period remained an open wound in French society. Many wanted them forgotten to bring about the necessary healing among all French people. Others, no less vocal, claimed that France had to acknowledge that dark episode. President François Mitterrand was a partisan of the former. It was left to his successor, Jacques Chirac, to declare openly upon his election in 1995 that France had to assume Vichy's guilt.

Memorial in Vienna depicting Jew scrubbing the street

V I E N N A

Capital of the Republic of AUSTRIA. Jews occupied a central place in the intellectual, cultural, and social life of the city from the late nineteenth century to the 1930s. There were 180,000 JEWS living there in the late 1920s. By the time of the ANSCHLUSS—the Nazi takeover of Austria on 12 March 1938—30,000 Jews fearing what the future would bring had left.

Anti-Jewish measures already being taken in GERMANY were immediately applied in Austria. They were aimed at first at pressuring the Jews into moving away by destroying their economic base. They also included humiliation—as Jewish men and

women were forced to wash the street. Next came denial of civil rights, arrests, pogroms, and massive "ARYANIZATION" of Jewish property. This led to the departure in a matter of months of some 50,000 Jews while hundreds of others committed suicide. Jewish institutions which had been closed and whose directors had been arrested were reopened. The directors were released when German authorities decided to use these institutions to speed up the flow of Jews out of the country.

After the outbreak of the war in September 1939, Jews who were still living in Vienna, had nowhere to go. They were concentrated in areas resembling

Jews forced to scrub streets, November 1938

GHETTOS and alternated between fear of frequent attacks and fear of DEPORTATION. They were all frantically looking for ways to escape. They turned to a number of Jewish organizations, such as the AMERICAN JEWISH JOINT DISTRIBUTION COMMITTEE (Joint) as well as representatives of the PALESTINE Jewish community secretly present in Vienna.

In 1941, mass deportations to DEATH CAMPS in POLAND, via THERESIENSTADT, were supervised by Alois BRUNNER. Less than 50,000 Jews remained in Vienna. Most of them, including the directors of Jewish institutions, were deported to their deaths. By late 1944, only some 6,000 Viennese Jews, most of them partners in "privileged mixed marriages" were still living in the city.

VILNA (Vilnius)

Capital of LITHUANIA. It was a major center of Jewish religious, cultural and political creativity. From 1920 it was under Polish rule. On the eve of the War more than a quarter of its 200,000 inhabitants were JEWS. On 16 September 1939, the Russian army took over Vilna. During the few weeks the Russians were there, many Jewish REFUGEES from POLAND made their way to Vilna in the expectation that it would soon be part of an independent Lithuania. When the Russians left Vilna on 28 October, after ceding it to Lithuania, there was a POGROM against the Jews conducted by Lithuanians, Poles, and criminal elements.

Some 15,000 refugees came to the city. These included intellectuals, leaders, and rabbis and students of Talmudic academies. In July 1940 Vilna was incorporated with the rest of Lithuania into SOVIET RUSSIA. Although the Jews were not subject to physical persecution, their activities were severely restricted (Jewish studies were forbidden as were organizations, parties, and any form of national expression). Moreover the Soviet economic regime severely undermined the livelihood of most Jews. During this period over 6,000 of the refugees managed to escape through Soviet Russia to the Far East, Palestine, and the United States.

All this ended when the Germans took over the city on 24 June 1941. Immediately anti-Jewish laws were issued and the Germans set up a JUDENRAT (Jewish Council). By July the EINSATZGRUPPEN, the Nazi action groups, were rounding up Jews and taking them to be shot in the nearby PONARY forest. In September, two adjacent GHETTOS were established and Jews herded into them. In a series of AKTIONS thousands of Jews were taken to Ponary and shot. By the end of the year, the Germans had killed over 33,000 out of the 57,000 Jews who had been in Vilna on their arrival. The smaller ghetto had been liquidated.

For most of 1942 there were no further aktions and the Jews were able to develop a flourishing life in the ghetto, despite the deprivations. The unusual concentration of outstanding individuals led to a rich cultural life as well as the growth of a strong UNDERGROUND, The FAREYNEGTE PARTIZANER ORGANIZATSYE (FPO, United Fighter's Organization) was established and from Vilna came the initial call for Jewish RESISTANCE (see Abba KOVNER). The Judenrat, headed by Jacob GENS, ran the ghetto efficiently and eventually 14,000 of the inmates had jobs. The assumption was that if the Germans found the ghetto economically worthwhile, they would not destroy it. During this quiet period the Judenrat cooperated with the underground.

In the spring of 1943, the mass killings recommenced. The FPO came into direct conflict with Gens and the Judenrat with the latter now fearing that the underground was endangering the ghetto population. This came to a head in July when Gens acceded to the German demand to hand over the underground commander, Yitzhak WITTENBERG, under the threat that failure to do so would mean the destruction of the ghetto. In fact the fate of the ghetto was already sealed. In August and September there were mass deportations, mainly to CONCENTRATION CAMPS in ESTONIA and LATVIA, others to Ponary and the SOBIBÓR DEATH CAMP. Hundreds of members of the underground escaped to the forests to maintain their resistance. Vilna was close to large forests and other partisans came there from different parts of Lithuania.

It was in July 1944 in the forests that Abba Kovner began the movement for "illegal" immigration to PALESTINE (Israel) that was to gather such momentum when the War was over. Apart from the partisans only a couple of thousand Vilna Jews somehow managed to survive the HOLOCAUST.

VISSER, LODEWIJK

(1871–1942) Judge, law professor and leading personality of Dutch Jewry. In 1915, Visser was appointed to the Supreme Court of the NETHERLANDS, and became its chairman in 1939. In the 1930s, he was involved in aid activities for REFUGEES and protests against the persecution of JEWS in GERMANY. When Jews were removed from the civil service in Holland after the Nazi occupation (autumn, 1940), he was dismissed from the Supreme Court. The Supreme Court itself decided not to oppose this act (voting was 12 in favor, 5 against).

In December 1940, Visser became chairman of the Jewish Coordination Committee (JCC), a new organization that tried to provide leadership to the Jewish community. In February 1941, he opposed the establishment of the Nazi-appointed Jewish Council (*Joodsche Raad*, see JUDENRAT). Afterward, he constantly challenged the Jewish Council. He brought several cases of major Jewish concern directly to the Dutch authorities. In October 1941, the JCC was disbanded by the Germans. Visser continued his activities and the Nazis warned him that he would be sent to a CONCENTRATION CAMP (13 February 1942). He died four days later from heart failure.

VOLKSDEUTSCHE

("German-folk")

German ethnic minorities scattered outside GERMANY, throughout east-central Europe. It was important to the Nazis to strengthen such communities.

When the Germans occupied POLAND, Polish citizens of German origin were registered. They became part of a privileged class. They were not subjected to many of the restrictions placed on the Polish population and were given a richer diet. Even in countries not directly occupied by the Germans, but allied with them, the Volksdeutsche enjoyed a special status. Many joined the German army. In

Portrait of Lodewijk Ernst Visser as the head of the Jewish Coordination Committee

1939–1940, in keeping with agreements made with SOVIET RUSSIA, German nationals were removed from territories taken over by Soviet Russia (the Baltic States, BESSARABIA, and northern BUKOVINA). Most were resettled in parts of Poland that had been merged with Germany and in the GENERALGOUVERNEMENT. By January 1944, some 770,000 Volksdeutsche had been resettled.

Volksdeutsche received a large portion of the personal property stolen from Jews sent to CONCENTRATION and DEATH CAMPS. On 15 December 1942, Heinrich HIMMLER decreed that "the entire real estate of Jews in the Generalgouvernement will be assigned to resettlers [i.e., Volksdeutsche] and other privileged applicants." Many Volksdeutsche were actively recruited into SS units and worked in the death camps.

However, instances have been recorded of persons of German ancestry participating in the struggle against Nazi Germany. The Nazi authorities regarded these people as traitors and treated them as such.

WALDHEIM, KURT

(1918–) Austrian military officer, later, secretary-general of the United Nations and president of AUSTRIA. Waldheim was a law student in VIENNA at the time of GERMANY's annexation of Austria. He became a member of the Nazi Student Association and joined the SA stormtroopers. He was drafted and fought in the Sudetenland, FRANCE and SOVIET RUSSIA. He was reassigned to the Balkans, where he fought against Yugoslav PARTISANS, and then as an intelligence officer in GREECE, at the time of the DEPORTATIONS of Greek Jews.

Waldheim's career following the war is certainly the strangest of any of the ex-Nazis. In 1947, he was included on the War Criminal List of the UNITED NATIONS WAR CRIMES COMMISSION by the Yugoslav government. He was never tried. He became an Austrian diplomat and rose to be foreign minister. In 1971, he was elected secretary-general of the United Nations, the very organization that listed him as a suspected war criminal! He was re-elected to a second term. In 1986, he was elected president of Austria. In 1987, the United States Justice Department listed Waldheim as a suspected war criminal. He was accused of being dishonest about his war record. In 1988, he was cleared by an international commission of historians of having direct responsibility for war crimes. However, in the same report, the commission found that Waldheim knew of the crimes and did nothing to stop them. The damaging report did not keep him from completing his term as president.

Kurt Waldheim second from left in uniform, in Yugoslavia, May 1943

WALLENBERG, RAOUL

(1913–?) Swedish diplomat who saved many Jews in BUDAPEST, HUNGARY. In March 1944, GERMANY occupied Hungary. The DEPORTATION of Hungarian JEWS to AUSCHWITZ began in May. Between 14 May and 8 July, 437,402 Jews were deported on 148 trains to Auschwitz. When the deportations were halted, only the 200,000 Jews of Budapest remained in Hungary.

In January 1944, United States President Franklin D. ROOSEVELT established the WAR REFUGEE BOARD. This organization tried to get help from other nations in protecting Hungarian Jews, the last remaining large Jewish community in Nazi-occupied Europe. Wal-

> *Whoever saves a single human life, saves the entire world.*
>
> *The Talmud*

lenberg was chosen to lead the rescue operation in Budapest. He was a Swedish aristocrat, from a distinguished banking family. Since he had studied at the University of Michigan, he knew many Americans. From his work as a banker in PALESTINE, he also knew Jews. Wallenberg was given a diplomatic passport and backing, a large sum of money, and freedom to use "unusual" methods to rescue Jews.

Wallenberg arrived in Budapest on 9 July 1944, the day after the deportations had been stopped. He knew that the Russian army was advancing and that Germany's defeat was only a matter of time.

He immediately began distributing impressive looking passports bearing the Swedish seal for Jews. The first 5,000 was only the beginning. The embassies of other neutral countries followed Wallenberg's lead. Carl LUTZ, an American-educated Swiss diplomat, led the efforts to save Jews on behalf of SWITZERLAND. Wallenberg also worked with local Jews and Jewish youth movements to set up hospitals, nurseries, and soup kitchens.

In November 1944, Adolf EICHMANN ordered the arrest of all Jewish men between the ages of 16 and 60. He marched them to the Austrian border in the first of a series of DEATH MARCHES. Wallenberg reacted immediately. He chased convoys carrying Jews, stopped trains about to depart for Auschwitz, and roamed through the city, demanding that German and Hungarian officers free the arrested Jews.

When threats did not work, he offered bribes, or even stood between Jews and their captors, saying they would have to take him first. Inside Budapest, he set up 31 hostels which gave refuge to 15,000 Jews. Wallenberg protected these houses and their occupants by giving them diplomatic status.

When the Soviet army entered Budapest on 16 January 1945, 100,000 Jews were still alive. Many, if not most of them, owed their lives to Wallenberg and his colleagues.

On 17 January 1945, Wallenberg was seen by Dr.

Passport of Raoul Wallenberg, 30 June 1944

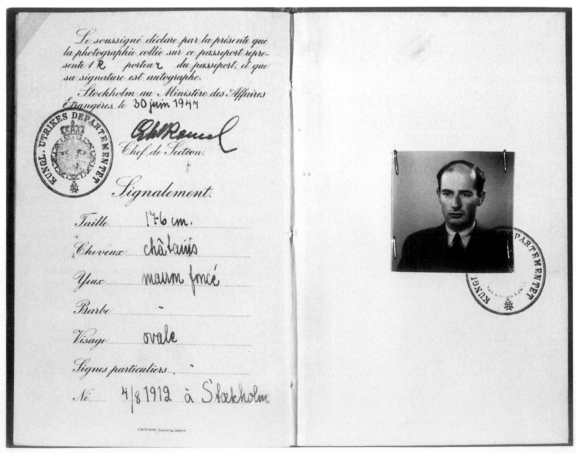

Erno Peto, one of his closest collaborators, in the company of Soviet soldiers. He said: "I do not know whether I am a guest of the Soviets or their prisoner." He was never seen as a free man again.

For 10 years, SOVIET RUSSIA denied that Wallenberg was in their custody. But after the death of Joseph STALIN, the Soviet Union formally announced that Wallenberg had indeed been arrested. They produced a death certificate to back up their claim that he had died of a heart attack in a Soviet prison in 1947.

Nevertheless, until the 1980s, there were occasional reports from former political prisoners who claimed that they had seen Wallenberg in various Soviet prisons. His fate may never be definitely known.

Wallenberg's bravery has been recognized in many ways. He was awarded honorary United States citizenship by Congress. His story has been told, streets have been named after him, and monuments have been erected in many places in the world.

WANNSEE CONFERENCE

Conference that decided the details of the Nazi mass murder of European Jewry. It was held in a villa on the edge of a BERLIN lake on 20 January 1942. Gathered at the table were 15 men, 7 of whom had doctorates. These were the state secretaries of the government offices that carried out most of the anti-Jewish policies. They represented the German Department of Justice, the Foreign Ministry, the GESTAPO, the SS Police, the Race and Resettlement Office, Adolf HITLER's office, the NAZI PARTY (see NATIONAL SOCIALIST GERMAN WORKERS' PARTY), the GENERALGOUVERNE-MENT of the Polish occupation, and the office in charge of distributing Jewish property. They were brought together by Reinhard HEYDRICH, head of the SS Reich Security Main Office (REICHSSICHERHEITSHAUPT-AMT), to announce a policy decision—the "FINAL SOLU-TION" to the "Jewish Problem"—that is the murder of all Jews in Europe. These men knew all about the Jewish policy. Their cooperation and that of their agencies was needed if the task was to be accomplished. The director of Heydrich's Jewish Office, Adolf EICHMANN, was present. He had helped prepare the conference and was later to testify about the

The villa in Wannsee, Berlin where the Wannsee Conference was held

Wannsee Conference at his trial in Jerusalem.

Heydrich stated the conference's aims:

Another possible solution of the Jewish problem has now taken the place of emigration, i.e., evacuation of the Jews to the East.... Such activities are, however, to be considered as provisional actions, but practical experience is already being collected, which is of greatest importance in relation to the future final solution of the Jewish problem.

Those at the conference fully understood what Heydrich was saying, even though he was using his language quite carefully. "Evacuation to the East" was a Nazi code-expression for DEPORTATION TO CONCENTRATION CAMPS. The "Final Solution" meant systematic murder. Those present viewed a chart detailing 11 million Jews (including those in countries not conquered by the Nazis) who were all destined for death. They debated "various possibilities for a solution," which Eichmann said at his trial meant different methods of killing. He recalled that it was a pleasant social occasion that ended with drinks and a luncheon.

Historians debate about exactly when the decision was made to kill all the JEWS and by whom. Most conclude that the real decision was made by Adolf Hitler more than a year earlier. However, beginning with the Wannsee Conference, the killing of all Jews, wherever they could be found, was the announced policy of the THIRD REICH. After the conference, the construction of the DEATH CAMPS began.

WAR REFUGEE BOARD (WRB)

Board established by President Franklin D. ROOSEVELT of the United States, in January 1944, to carry out the American policy on rescue of JEWS in Nazi Europe. It was established in response to an urgent request by Secretary of the Treasury Henry J. MORGENTHAU, Jr.

On 16 January 1944, Morgenthau met with Roosevelt and presented him with "A Personal Report to the President." It described the State Department's efforts to prevent rescue attempts and discourage the acceptance of refugees by the UNITED STATES. Morgenthau presented a proposal for actively involving the United States in rescue activities. Within days of the meeting, Roosevelt established the War Refugee Board. Its members were the secretaries of state, treasury, and war. Most of the money for the Board's work had to come from private sources. The president allocated $1 million; American Jewish organizations, most especially the AMERICAN JEWISH JOINT DISTRIBUTION COMMITTEE, contributed $17 million.

The WRB was directed by John PEHLE, a Treasury Department lawyer who had helped Morgenthau alert the president about the American government's "acceptance" of the Jewish plight. The WRB set out to try to find a haven for Jews. It tried to remove Jews and other persecuted people from territories held by the Nazis. It also sought to find places where they could be sent. It tried to send supplies to CONCENTRATION CAMPS. It threatened Nazi leaders that they would be tried for CRIMES AGAINST HUMANITY if they participated in the murder of Jews.

The WRB lobbied for statements from Roosevelt condemning the murder of Jews. It drew up plans for postwar TRIALS OF WAR CRIMINALS and argued for the bombing of AUSCHWITZ (see AUSCHWITZ BOMBING). It also established a small camp for refugees in the United States at FORT ONTARIO, Oswego, New York.

The WRB funded the work of people like the Swedish diplomat Raoul WALLENBERG, who saved perhaps as many as 200,000 Jews. Yet, when John Pehle viewed the work of the WRB after 12 years of American efforts, he commented: "What we did was little enough. It was late. Late and little, I would say." Still the work of the WRB, however limited, was valuable.

W   A   R   S   A   W

Capital of POLAND. Out of a total population of one million, in 1939, more than 350,000 of its inhabitants were JEWS—the largest Jewish community after New York. It was a bustling center of Jewish life and culture.

The city fell to the Germans at the end of September 1939, and soon after, the German began to herd all the Jews into a GHETTO. Thirty percent of the city's population was crammed into 2.4 percent of its area. At its peak the Ghetto was home to almost half-a-million Jews. By November 1940 the ghetto was completely surrounded by a wall and sealed off.

The Germans appointed a JUDENRAT (Jewish Council) headed by Adam CZERNIAKOW, which was responsible for running the ghetto—under close German supervision. It also supplied workers to the Germans for FORCED LABOR. The Judenrat was divided into many departments including supervision of a Jewish police force. Life in the ghetto was horrorific. Food rations were minimal and inhabitants died of starvation and disease in large numbers—in 1941 a tenth of the population (over 40,000 persons) died in the ghetto. Smuggling became a way of life to augment food supplies and many ingenious ways were found to get in food from outside. Young CHILDREN became expert in going down into the sewers and emerging outside the ghetto and somehow obtaining food to bring back. These little children became among the most important people in the ghetto. If they were discovered smuggling in food, they were shot. With the influx of more and more Jews into the ghetto, brought in from outside Warsaw, the situation grew increasingly grave. The daily bread ration was down to a mere four ounces.

Despite the terrible situation, the Jews against all odds and with great courage attempted to maintain a sense of normalcy. Each housing block had a committee to look after its members. Soup kitchens were established to distribute food. Orphanages were created for those who had lost their parents (the most famous was that headed by

According to the laws of nature, we ought to have been annihilated. But we do not conform to the laws of nature. A certain invisible power is embedded in us and preserves our will to live. We don't have cases of suicide. the beaten-down, shamed, broken Jews of Poland love life. They do not wish to disappear from the earth before their time.

From "Scroll of Agony" a diary written in the ghetto by the educator Chaim A. Kaplan.

Janusz KORSCZAK). The Judenrat taxed the better-off so as to help those in worse situation. Schools were created for both children and adults. Youth groups, especially the Zionist YOUTH MOVEMENTS, were established. Cultural programs provided entertainment, such as concerts, plays and poetry readings—which for a short time too the audience's minds off what was happening around them. Synagogues, rabbis and religious life served as important anchors for the observant. The festivals were kept. Study was

pursued and the historian Emanuel RINGELBLUM founded an archive to document all aspects of the ghetto. A political underground produced a secret press. The community fought for its soul, refusing to be beaten down into animals and exhibited a will to live and a hunger to learn (see box).

In the summer of 1942, more then 30,000 Jews were rounded up in the ghetto and marched to the UMSCHLAGPLATZ (assembly point) and transported in cattle carts to the TREBLINKA, DEATH CAMP, some sixty miles away. By that time, word had reached the ghetto of the fate of other communities and they realized their fate. The task of rounding up the Jews fell to the Jewish police who, together with a force of SS Latvian soldiers, and German and Ukrainian police, isolated block after block, street after street, and finally building after building as they rounded up the inhabitants. The Judenrat had been told to organize the deportations and in desperation Adam Czerniaków committed suicide, writing in his diary "The SS wants me to kill children with my own hands." The UNDERGROUND at this time decided to form a JEWISH FIGHTING ORGANIZATION but were not yet ready for action.

Jews under arrest after being taken out of underground bunkers in the Warsaw Ghetto Uprising

By September 1942 only 50,000 Jews remained in the ghetto. The Jewish Fighting Organization issued a proclamation of resistance (see WARSAW GHETTO UPRISING). On 9 January 1943 Heinrich HIMMLER visited the ghetto and ordered the DEPORTATION of another 8,000 Jews.

The Jews were in hiding and the underground went into action. They attacked German troops in the dark hallways of buildings and the German troops were unwilling to go down to the cellars. After a few days the operation was called off after 5,000–6,000 ghetto residents had been deported. Those who remained believed that the RESISTANCE had ended the deportations. They now fortified their positions and began to construct bunkers and shelters below ground so as to be ready for the next fight. This broke out on the eve of Passover, April 1943. For the story of this uprising see WARSAW GHETTO UPRISING.

When Warsaw was finally liberated by the Soviet army on 17 January 1945, 300 Jews were found hiding in the non-Jewish parts of the city. The ghetto had been razed and of all the historic sites of pre-war Warsaw there remained only one synagogue—and the cemetery.

WARSAW GHETTO UPRISING

Last desperate act of RESISTANCE by survivors in the WARSAW GHETTO. Between July and September 1942, 265,000 Jews were deported from Warsaw to the DEATH CAMP of TREBLINKA. After this, only 50,000 Jews remained in the ghetto. The old and the very young had been deported and those who remained were mostly young, able-bodied, and without families. They were furious at themselves because they had not resisted.

Despair soon gave way to resistance. The JEWISH FIGHTING ORGANIZATION, the ZOB (Zydowska Organizacja Bojowa), took control of the ghetto. It proclaimed:

> Jewish masses, the hour is drawing near. You must be prepared to resist. Not a single Jew should go to the railroad cars. Those who are unable to put up active resistance should resist passively, should go into hiding.
>
> Our slogan must be: All are ready to die as human beings.

When SS Chief Heinrich HIMMLER visited Warsaw and ordered the DEPORTATION of 8,000 Jews, ghetto residents thought this was the end. Resistance

Jews jumping from blazing building during the Warsaw Ghetto Uprising

GERMAN REPORT ON WARSAW GHETTO UPRISING

19 April 1943. Ghetto sealed off from 3:00 hours. At 6:00 hours deployment of the Waffen ss for the combing of the remainder of the ghetto. Immediately upon entry strong concerted fire by the Jews and bandits.

We succeeded in forcing the enemy to withdraw from the roof-tops and strong-points situated in high positions to the cellars or bunkers and sewers. Shock patrols were then deployed against known bunkers with the task of clearing out the occupants and destroying the bunkers. The presence of Jews in the sewers was established. Total flooding was carried out, rendering presence impossible.

22 April 1943. It is unfortunately impossible to prevent a proportion of the bandits and Jews from hiding in the sewers under the ghetto where they have evaded capture by preventing the flooding. The city administration is not in a position to remove this inconvenience. Smoke-bombs and mixing creosote with the water have also failed to achieve the desired result.

23 April 1943. The whole Aktion [operation] is made more difficult by the cunning tricks employed by the Jews and bandits, e.g., it was discovered that live Jews were being taken to the Jewish cemetery in the corps carts that collect the dead bodies lying around, and were thus escaping from the ghetto.

24 April 1943. At 18:15 hours the search party entered the buildings after they had been cordoned off and established the presence of a large number of Jews. As most of these Jews resisted I gave the order to burn them out. Not until the whole street and all the courtyards on both sides were in flames did the Jews, some of them on fire, come out from the blocks of buildings or try to save themselves by jumping from the windows and balconies into the street onto which they had thrown beds, blankets, and other things. Time and time again it could be observed that Jews and bandits preferred to return into the flames rather than fall into our hands.

8 May 1943. There must still be about 3,000 to 4,000 Jews in the underground cavities, sewers, and bunkers. The undersigned is determined not to terminate this Aktion until the very last Jew is destroyed.

10 May 1943. The resistance put up by the Jews today was unabated. In contrast to previous days, the members of the Jewish main fighter groups still in existence and not destroyed have apparently retreated to the highest ruins accessible to them in order to inflict casualties on the raiding parties by firing on them.

13 May 1943. For two days the few Jews and criminals still in the ghetto have been making use of the hiding places still provided by the ruins to return at night to the bunkers known to them, eating there and supplying themselves with food for the next day.

16 May 1943. The former Jewish quarter of Warsaw is no longer in existence. With the blowing up of the Warsaw Synagogue, the Aktion was terminated at 20:15 hours....

Total number of Jews caught or verifiable exterminated: 56,065.

From the reports of SS General Jürgen Stroop, in charge of the German Forces

sprang into action. There were battles in the streets near the UMSCHLAGPLATZ (the deportation point). The deportation soon ended. Full credit for the halt was given to the resistance. Actually, Himmler had only ordered a thinning out of the ghetto.

On 18 April 1943, the ghetto received word that an operation was soon to take place which would take away its inhabitants. The population was alerted immediately.

The Warsaw Ghetto Uprising began on 19 April 1943, on the second night of Passover. It continued for more than a month until the ghetto was destroyed by fire and almost all its inhabitants were killed or captured (some escaped through the sewers into places in Warsaw, outside the ghetto).

At 6:00 a.m. on 19 April, Colonel von Sammern initiated the operation. Almost the entire Jewish population was in hiding places and bunkers. Within 90 minutes, German troops were attacked by Molotov cocktails and sent fleeing. The Jewish fighters were thrilled: German supermen had fallen.

On 20 April, the Germans attacked the factory area where five Jewish resistance fighter squads were stationed. A mine was set off and again the Germans were forced to retreat. When they reappeared, Jewish fighters opened fire. Hand to hand fighting followed. The Germans raised a white flag. The Jews answered with gunfire.

The Germans cut off electricity, water, and gas to the ghetto. Police dogs were brought in to uncover shelters. On the third day, the Germans no longer entered the ghetto in large groups. Small bands roamed throughout the ghetto. The Jewish resistance also broke into small mobile squads. The Germans who had planned to liquidate the ghetto within three days now decided to burn it down block by block. The Jews held out for more than a month.

The Uprising was literally a revolution in Jewish history. Its importance does not lie in the result, which was the slaughter of the Jews. Those who fought saw themselves as freedom fighters, willing to risk all, to lose all, yet not to surrender.

The most important sense of the Warsaw Ghetto Uprising was given by its 24-year-old commander, Mordechai ANIELEWICZ, who wrote to Yitzhak ZUCKERMAN, a unit commander:

> What really matters is that the dream of my life has become true.
>
> Jewish self defense in the Warsaw ghetto has become a fact. Jewish armed resistance and retaliation have become a reality. I have been witness to the magnificent heroic struggle of the Jewish fighters.

W A R T H E G A U

(or "Wartheland")

A territory created in October 1939 in the region of POLAND that was incorporated into the Nazi Reich. Its name came from the river Warthe and *Gau* ("district"). It was the largest administrative district in the Reich, covering nearly 17,000 square miles.

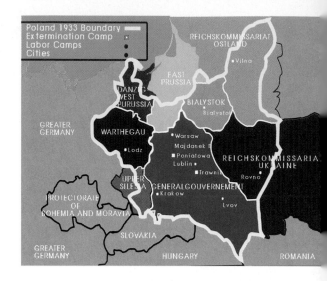

The Warthegau was divided into three districts (Posen, Hohensalza, and Kalisz) and forty-four subdistricts. Its administrative head (*Gauleiter*) was Artur Greiser. He viewed his territory as a testing ground for ways of dealing with population "problems." For this reason, the Warthegau contained the DEATH CAMP of CHELMNO, where more than 150,000 Polish Jews were murdered in gas vans (see GAS CHAMBERS, GAS VANS, AND CREMATORIA). Almost 400,000 Jews in the territory were put to death and a mere 5,000 survived. It ceased to exist after its liberation by the Soviet army in January 1945.

W E H R M A C H T

("Defense Force")

Name of the German armed forces after compulsory military service was introduced in 1935. The Wehrmacht was heavily influenced by old German military traditions. These traditions had been a major cause for German expansionism before and during World War I. The leaders of the Wehrmacht were members of the old German ruling class. They shared most of the basic aims of the Nazi government. Adolf HITLER and his generals together prepared GERMANY for another world war. From 100,000 men, in 1935, the army grew by the summer of 1939 to 2.7 million soldiers. Without the German army, the HOLOCAUST would have been impossible. Outside the DEATH CAMPS, it was in many cases the Wehrmacht and not the SS that performed the mass killings of JEWS and other victims.

The execution of Polish hostages in retaliation for an attack on a German police station by members of the under-ground organization "White Eagle." In all, 51 residents of Bochnia were shot in Uzbornia Forest by the Wehrmacht

WEIMAR REPUBLIC

First German republic which existed between the end of World War I in November 1918 and the rise to power of the NATIONAL SOCIALISTS (Nazis) in January 1933. Previously GERMANY had been a monarchy. The democratic republic took its name from the town of Weimar, where its Constitutional Assembly first met in February 1919. The beginnings of the republic were unstable, with short-lived revolutionary governments in a few German states. There was also a serious economic crisis which led to the enormous inflation of 1923. Between 1924 and 1929, the Republic entered a period of relative calm and stability. Its last few years were again rocked by political instability, high unemployment, and street violence. Between 1930 and 1933, the tremendous gains of the Communist and National Socialist parties prevented the formation of a democratic majority in the German parliament, the REICHSTAG. All govern-

ments during those years were minority governments appointed by President Paul von HINDENBURG. Hindenburg was himself a supporter of the old monarchical ways.

For over half a million JEWS in Germany, the Weimar Republic meant both unequalled opportunities and new threats. After 1918, for the first time, Jews became minister of foreign affairs, President of the Prussian Academy of the Arts, and President of a German University. There was a renaissance of Jewish cultural life. German Jews were represented widely in Weimar Germany's vibrant cultural élite during the so-called "Golden Twenties." At the same time, ANTISEMITISM was a major feature in the political life of the Weimar Republic. The highest ranking Jewish official in German politics, Walther Rathenau, was assassinated by right-wing terrorists only a few weeks after his appointment as foreign minister in 1922. Jews (and Social Democrats) were held responsible in right-wing circles for Germany's defeat in World War I, which they regarded a "stab in the back" by internal enemies rather than a military defeat on the battleground.

Adolf HITLER's National Socialist German Workers Party caused political uproar for the first time with its failed attempt to seize power in Munich in November 1923. After receiving a mild sentence by a court system that many felt favored the right wing, Hitler worked to overthrow the Weimar Republic using democratic means. While his party never succeeded in gaining the absolute majority of votes, it became the largest party in the Reichstag. After initial hesitation, President von Hindenburg appointed Hitler Chancellor on 30 January 1933. Hitler's dictatorship meant the end of the Weimar Republic.

WEISSMANDEL, MICHAEL BER

(1903–1956) Slovak orthodox rabbi, leader of UNDER-GROUND rescue efforts. Immediately after the first DE-PORTATIONS of Jews from SLOVAKIA to occupied POLAND, Weissmandel attempted to smuggle food and supplies into the CAMPS. He employed non-Jewish couri-

Michael Ber Weissmandel

> *Whoever met this man for the first time —a man whose face was fringed with a wild black beard and long sidelocks and whose neglected appearance hardly made an appealing impression—could not imagine the personality hidden behind this exterior. His operations in the* WORKING GROUP *defied the rules of logic. Did it not require the Partisan Rabbi's creative imagination, courage and wonderful lack of a realistic outlook on practical issues?*
>
> *Oskar Neumann*
> *Slovak Zionist leader*

ers for the task. Weissmandel was a leader of the Bratislava "WORKING GROUP" a group of Jewish activists who organized secretly to save Slovak Jews. Under the Working Group, factories and workshops were opened in three camps, employing 300,000 Jewish prisoners. Weissmandel initiated the EUROPA PLAN, which worked by bribing Nazi officials in order to influence them to free Jews. He exchanged letters secretly with Jewish leaders in the free world, whom he bitterly attacked for their failure to rescue the endangered Jews of Europe. In the spring of 1944, Weissmandel warned Hungarian Jewish leaders of the Germans' plans for their deportation. His warnings were ignored. He also begged Jews in western countries to demand that AUSCHWITZ and the railway tracks leading to it be bombed (see AUSCHWITZ BOMBING). In the summer of 1944, he was arrested and placed aboard a train heading for Auschwitz. On the journey, Weissmandel managed to jump off the train and went into hiding. After the war he settled in the United States.

WEIZMANN, CHAIM

(1874–1952) Zionist statesman, the first president of the State of ISRAEL.

Born in Russia, Weizmann studied chemistry in GERMANY and SWITZERLAND. While still in his twenties, he was regarded as a leading figure in the Zionist movement. In 1903, he went to Manchester University and played a key role in obtaining British recognition of PALESTINE as a Jewish national home. From

1920 to 1931 and 1935 to 1946, he was the president of the World Zionist Organization.

When war loomed in Europe in the late 1930's, Weizmann concentrated his diplomacy on the rescue of JEWS from Nazi Germany and their absorption in Palestine. He attempted to use his strong ties with British policy makers to promote this cause. His success was limited since the British felt they had to appease the Arabs. In 1937, Weizmann supported the plan of the British Royal Commission to partition Palestine between the Jews and Arabs, and create a Jewish state. However, he became strongly critical of British policy with the publication of the May 1939 WHITE PAPER, which limited Jewish immigration to Palestine, banned the sale of land to Jews, and doomed the Jewish community to the status of permanent minority in Palestine.

During WORLD WAR II, he worked for the creation of a JEWISH BRIGADE GROUP in the Allied forces, which was finally achieved in 1944. At the end of the war, the British government continued to appease the Arabs at the expense of the Jews, ignoring the HOLOCAUST and its survivors. GREAT BRITAIN resisted American efforts to have at least 100,000 survivors admitted to Palestine. Despite his disappointment at this British move, Weizmann rejected David BEN-GURION's activist policy of military resistance. Weizmann feared it would open the Jews of Palestine to British repression and later Arab reprisal. From 1946 to 1948, he participated in the final struggle for the creation of the State of Israel and in February 1949 he was elected the first president of that State.

WEIZSÄCKER, ERNST VON

(1882–1951) Secretary of State in the German Foreign Office under Joachim von RIBBENTROP, and German ambassador to the Vatican from 1943.

Although Weizsäcker considered Adolf HITLER too extreme, he never expressed his opposition very strongly and faithfully executed Nazi policies. He was fully aware of the persecution of the JEWS and received copies of the reports of the EINSATZGRUPPEN and the WANNSEE CONFERENCE.

Weizsäcker was convicted after the war for CRIMES AGAINST HUMANITY. This was because he had failed to object to Adolf EICHMANN's requests for DEPORTATIONS of Jews from German-occupied countries to AUSCHWITZ.

Ernst von Weizsäcker

He served only 18 months of the 5-year prison sentence imposed on him at his postwar trial.

Over 30 years later, his son, Richard von Weizsäcker, became president of GERMANY. He became the voice of German conscience over the Holocaust and proclaimed that "our forefathers have left us a heavy legacy."

Time after time, he spoke of the shame of Germany for the Holocaust and the need to remember it constantly so that it may never recur.

> *It is not a matter of overcoming the past: One can do no such thing. The past does not allow itself to be retrospectively altered or undone. But whoever closes his eyes to the past becomes blind to the present. Whoever does not wish to remember inhumanity becomes susceptible to the dangers of new infection.*
>
> German President Richard von Weizsächer, 50 years after the Holocaust. "The World Must Know," Washington Holocaust Museum, p. 223

W E S T E R B O R K

Transit CONCENTRATION CAMP through which the majority of Dutch JEWS was deported to the DEATH CAMPS in eastern Europe. It was located in the northeastern Dutch province of Drenthe. Originally, Westerbork housed German Jewish refugees who had entered the NETHERLANDS illegally after KRISTALLNACHT (November 1938).

At the end of 1941, the German authorities decided to use Westerbork as one of three transit camps in western Europe (the others were Mechelen/Malines in BELGIUM and DRANCY in FRANCE). From 14 July 1942, Jews were assembled there as part of the "FINAL SOLUTION." The first DEPORTATION to AUSCHWITZ left on 15 July. Almost 100,000 Jews were deported from Westerbork: 54,930 to Auschwitz, 34,313 to SOBIBÓR, 4,771 to THERESIENSTADT, and 3,762 to BERGEN-BELSEN. The camp was liberated in April 1945, and at the time 876 Jews were still imprisoned there.

Joop Westerweel

W E S T E R W E E L ,   J O O P

(1899–1944) Non-Jewish Dutch teacher and rescuer of Jews. He was awarded the "RIGHTEOUS AMONG THE NATIONS" title by YAD VASHEM after his death.

Westerweel taught in Biulhoven, at a school which had taken in a large number of German Jewish refugee children in the 1930s. There he became aware of the plight of the JEWS. In 1942, when DEPORTATIONS of Dutch Jews to the DEATH CAMPS began, Westerweel became involved in organizing a group of young Zionist pioneers into an UNDERGROUND

Dutch Jews being boarded on a train to Westerbork from where they were sent to Auschwitz and Sobibór

movement. First, 49 pioneers were placed in hiding places in August 1942. Then, ways were explored to get the group out of Nazi-occupied Europe through BELGIUM and FRANCE to SWITZERLAND and SPAIN. Westerweel was central to the group in many ways because of his being—together with his wife and some other non-Jewish friends—the non-Jewish anchor of the underground. In February 1943, he personally directed a group of pioneers to the Franco-Spanish border (in the Pyrenees Mountains). On 11 March 1944, he was arrested by the Germans while trying to smuggle two pioneer girls over the NETHERLANDS-Belgium border. He was imprisoned and tortured in a CONCENTRATION CAMP. On 11 August 1944, he was executed.

WHITE PAPER OF 1939

A White Paper is a British government statement of policy. On 17 May 1939, the British Colonial Secretary, Malcolm MacDonald, presented the latest in a series of White Papers. These had set out GREAT BRITAIN's changing attitude towards Zionism since the time of the Balfour Declaration (2 November 1917). The Balfour Declaration's promise to establish in PALESTINE a national home for the Jewish people did not—according the 1939 White Paper—mean a sovereign Jewish state. It also imposed limitations on the expansion of the Jewish national home and on immigration of Jewish refugees. Only 75,000 immigrants would be let in during the five years that followed. After that time there would be no Jewish immigration at all without Arab consent. For the Zionist leaders this was seen as the British giving in to the "Arab revolt" that had been going on in Palestine from 1936 to 1939. This had included frequent Arab riots and a boycott of Jewish goods and services. In view of the threat to Jews in Europe, the Zionist leader Chaim WEIZMANN called it a "death sentence." An official statement by the JEWISH AGENCY FOR PALESTINE condemned any attempt to set up a permanent Arab majority rule over a Jewish minority in their ancestral and historical homeland. When war broke out, Palestinian Jews responded in two ways: by joining the British army to fight the Nazis and also by continuing with "illegal" immigration from Nazi Europe (see ALIYAH BET). As the Palestinian Jewish leader David BEN-GURION said, "We shall fight the war (against Nazism) as if there were no White Paper and we shall fight the White Paper as if there were no war!"

WHITE ROSE

A German RESISTANCE group, organized and led by college students. Its leaders were Hans Scholl, his sister Sophie, and Christoph Probst. It was the only German resistance group that protested the treatment of JEWS. The students were guided by a philosophy professor, Kurt Huber. Huber was an expert in the thought of Immanuel Kant, the 18th-century German moral philosopher who taught that human beings must never be used as a means to an end.

In 1942, they distributed leaflets calling for spiritual resistance. They said: "Every people deserves the government it is willing to endure."

The White Rose consisted of a network of students in Munich, HAMBURG, Freiburg, BERLIN, and

> *You shall act as if on you and on your deeds depended the fate of all Germany and you alone must answer for it.*
>
> *final words of Professor Kurt Huber*

Demonstration against the White Paper, in Tel Aviv, May 1939

VIENNA. In February 1943, they mounted an anti-Nazi demonstration in Munich. The group's leaders were executed on February 18, after they were betrayed by a university janitor. Just before his death, Scholl said: "Hold out in protest of all dictatorship."

Professor Huber was also arrested and executed.

WIESEL, ELIE

(1928–) Writer, whose books and lectures have helped bring the subject of the HOLOCAUST to the attention of the world.

Elie Wiesel is a survivor of the Holocaust who was born in Marametei, TRANSYLVANIA. He and his family were taken to the AUSCHWITZ death camp in 1944. In 1945, he was freed from the BUCHENWALD concentration camp, to which he had been transferred, and began writing as a journalist. In 1956, Wiesel published his most famous novel, *Night*, dealing with his own experiences in the Holocaust.

Wiesel has written many works on various aspects of Jewish life, but the major focus of his writings has been the Holocaust. His eyewitness approach and his gift for storytelling have made the history of the Holocaust accessible to millions of people. He has also tackled broad moral questions, including the difficulty of maintaining faith after the Holocaust.

Wiesel has spoken out against human atrocities and victimization around the world, while reserving a unique place for the Holocaust. His concern for

> *Listen to the silent screams of terrified mothers, listen to the prayers of anguished old men and women, listen to the tears of Jewish children, beautiful looking girls among them, with golden hair, whose vulnerable tenderness never left me...look and listen as the victims quietly walk towards dark flames so gigantic that the planet itself seemed in danger.*
>
> Excerpt from speech delivered by Elie Wiesel at commemorative ceremony for the 50th anniversary of the liberation of Auschwitz, 26 January 1995

human rights and his exceptional efforts in educating the world about the Holocaust earned him the Medal of Honor of the United States Congress in 1985. He received the Nobel Prize for Peace in 1986.

WIESENTHAL CENTER

See SIMON WIESENTHAL CENTER.

WIESENTHAL, SIMON

(1908–) Nazi hunter. In 1939, Simon Wiesenthal, an architect by training, lived in LVOV, POLAND. He and his family were deported, and Wiesenthal was sent to several labor and CONCENTRATION CAMPS, most notably BUCHENWALD and MAUTHAUSEN. He survived and, after the war, he volunteered to work in the War Crimes section of the U.S. Army in AUSTRIA. In 1947, he set up the Jewish Historical Documentation center in Linz, Austria, but lack of public interest and funding led to its closing in 1947.

In 1961, he opened the Jewish Documentation Center, in VIENNA. This was instrumental in tracing many Nazi war criminals and bringing them to justice. In 1980, he was awarded a gold medal for humanitarian work by the Congress of the United States. It was presented to him by President Jimmy Carter, who praised him "for keeping alive the

Simon Weisenthal

flame of justice in the world." In 1977, the Simon WIESENTHAL CENTER for the Holocaust was opened in his honor in Los Angeles.

The life of Simon Wiesenthal was made into a film based on his memoirs, "Murderers Among Us," with Ben Kingsley in the role of Wiesenthal.

WILNER, ARIE

(1917–1943) Jewish RESISTANCE leader in POLAND.

Before WORLD WAR II, Wilner was a member of Ha-Shomer ha-Tzair ("The Young Guard") Zionist YOUTH MOVEMENT in WARSAW. Immediately after the German occupation of Poland in September 1939, Wilner, along with many other youth group leaders, fled to VILNA in LITHUANIA.

In Vilna he continued his Zionist youth activities. These came to a sudden stop when the Germans occupied Lithuania in June 1941. Wilner managed to escape. He chose not to flee to freedom in eastern SOVIET RUSSIA, but rather to return to Warsaw, where the Jews had been forced into a GHETTO. He wanted to warn fellow Jews of the mass murder that he saw in Lithuania. He was among the first to bring word of this to Poland.

Once back in Poland, Wilner became a leading figure in the Jewish UNDERGROUND. He traveled from ghetto to ghetto. The situation for Jews in the Polish ghettos became desperate during the summer of 1942. This was when the mass DEPORTATIONS of 300,000 Jews began. They were sent from the Warsaw ghetto mostly to the DEATH CAMP at TREBLINKA. At this point, Wilner and others decided that armed resistance had to be the main means of fighting the Nazis. This would be either for the sake of survival, or at least for the chance to die with honor. In the summer of 1942, he was among the founders of the JEWISH FIGHTING ORGANIZATION (ZOB) in Warsaw. Wilner was experienced in traveling in disguise. He therefore became one of the major ZOB contacts with the Poles. Wilner used every possible means to obtain weapons for Jewish underground fighters in the ghetto. He was able to contact representatives of the underground Polish Home Army in the non-Jewish part of Warsaw.

Wilner arranged the Polish Home Army's official recognition of the ZOB. However, this did not lead to the supply of enough weapons for the ghetto.

Arie Wilner

Wilner therefore also made contact with members of the communist underground in Poland.

He participated in the uprising in Warsaw in January 1943. At that time, a group from the Zionist youth movement broke into a crowd of JEWS being assembled for deportation, and opened fire on SS men.

On 6 March 1943, the GESTAPO entered Wilner's apartment on the non-Jewish side of Warsaw. Wilner was posing as a Pole, but was arrested for possession of arms. The Nazis thought he was a member of the Polish underground. The Gestapo interrogated and tortured him to try to discover his contacts, but Wilner did not give any information on his colleagues.

After a short time, the Germans discovered that Wilner was a Jew. They deported him to a CONCENTRATION CAMP near Warsaw. Soon after, he was rescued by a member of the Polish Catholic Scouts Movement. Wilner returned secretly to the Warsaw ghetto in order to participate in the last resistance activities.

The WARSAW GHETTO UPRISING began on 19 April 1943. Despite having a wounded leg, Wilner took an active role in the fighting. He was inside the ZOB command bunker when the Germans discovered it. Wilner called on his comrades to commit suicide and died in the bunker.

WISE, STEPHEN SAMUEL

(1874–1949) Reform Rabbi, Jewish and Zionist leader in the United States. In 1915, Stephen Wise founded the American Jewish Congress to protect Jewish rights and fight discrimination against Jews, blacks and other minorities. Beginning in 1933, he mobilized JEWS and non-Jews in the fight against the Nazis, organized the boycott of Nazi GERMANY (see BOYCOTTS, ANTI-NAZI), and of the 1936 Berlin Olympics. As a member of President Franklin ROOSEVELT's Advisory Committee on REFUGEES, he devoted his energies and used his influence to try to save Jews from the Nazis. However, immigration to the United States was restricted and exceptions were only made for prominent scientists, writers, musicians and politicians.

His pleas for increased immigration to the United States and PALESTINE fell on deaf ears. As the grim reality of the HOLOCAUST unfolded, Wise negotiated persistently with his personal friend, President Roosevelt. These efforts were frustrated by the indifference and often deliberate obstruction of the State Department and other branches of the United States government. He was seldom able to break through these obstacles. In desperation, Wise organized the "Stop Hitler Now" demonstration on 1 March 1943. Twenty thousand people gathered in Madison Square Garden, and another 10,000 outside, to hear messages from Roosevelt, Winston CHURCHILL, and church and lay leaders. Wise's continuous efforts seem to have been tiresome even for Roosevelt: his archives contain a letter from Wise, on which Roosevelt had scrawled "keep the Rabbi out of my hair." Yet, Wise became a legendary figure among the Jews of Europe: U.S. dollars reaching the Jewish UNDERGROUND, were called "Stefans" in his honor.

WISLICENY, DIETER

(1911–1948) SS officer, Adolf EICHMANN's deputy at the Jewish affairs desk of the Reich Security Main Office (see REICHSSICHERHEITSHAUPTAMT).

Wisliceny was considered an expert in Jewish matters and, from September 1940, he acted as an advisor to the Slovakian government on Jewish policy. He gained a reputation for his efficiency in "freeing" SLOVAKIA of Jews, by deporting them to their deaths at AUSCHWITZ. This led to his participation in similar DEPORTATIONS of Jews from GREECE in 1943, and from HUNGARY in 1944. In Hungary, Wisli-

Stephen Samuel Wise

Dieter Wisliceny

ceny also took part in the negotiations with the Allies involving the exchange of goods for Jewish lives. He was a key witness at the NUREMBERG TRIAL, where he testified that Eichmann had informed him that the total number of Jews murdered was around 5 million. Wisliceny was tried and executed in Bratislava, Slovakia.

WITTENBERG, YITZHAK (ITZIK)

(1907–1943) The first commander of the FAREYNEGTE PARTIZANER ORGANIZATSYE (FPO), a Jewish RESISTANCE organization in the VILNA GHETTO. A dedicated communist, Wittenberg was a tailor by trade. When Vilna was occupied by the Germans on 21 June 1941, he became the leader of the ghetto and one of the founders of the FPO. He succeeded in organizing the arming of the FPO UNDERGROUND by obtaining weapons from German armories and having them smuggled into the ghetto.

Exactly what happened at the time of his capture and death is not clear. What is known is that he was betrayed and then arrested inside the ghetto by the Germans. The Germans were then attacked by ghetto fighters, who rescued their leader. Wittenberg went into hiding inside the ghetto. However,

the SS delivered a deadly order to the JUDENRAT (the Jewish Council in the ghetto). The SS demanded that either Wittenberg give himself up or they would kill all the inhabitants of the ghetto. This led to a bitter conflict inside the ghetto between the PARTISANS, who wanted to fight, and a majority of the inmates, who were afraid. In the end, Wittenberg decided to give himself up to prevent unnecessary bloodshed. He surrendered to the Judenrat on 16 July 1943, was handed over to the Germans and died on the same day. Some say he committed suicide, others that he was tortured to death by the GESTAPO.

WOMEN IN THE HOLOCAUST

All JEWS were targets for destruction in the Holocaust, but women were often subject to special horrors. Although the experience was horrible for both men and women, the nature of the persecutions were frequently different. Women SS guards were trained to supervise and terrorize women prisoners.

Jewish women were in double jeopardy during the Holocaust. Since they were Jewish, the Nazis considered them a danger to the "purity" of German society. In addition, since they were the ones to

Women prisoners after having their hair shorn, Auschwitz

bear children, women were especially targeted to ensure that a new generation of JEWS would not be born. Although accurate statistics are not available, it is thought that a higher proportion of women than men were murdered by the Nazis. For example, at AUSCHWITZ even women who were suitable for work were usually sent immediately to their deaths if they were accompanied by young CHILDREN. Able-bodied men were kept alive.

Jewish women were subject to the same Nazi persecutions as were men: they were forced into GHETTOS, into hiding, into CONCENTRATION CAMPS, and DEATH CAMPS. They were starved and tortured. In addition, many were raped, forced into prostitution, sterilized, and made to watch their children put through unimaginable suffering. Some who managed to avoid the camps joined PARTISAN and RESISTANCE movements.

Within the camp system, women and men were segregated. Camps for women opened at Maringen between 1933 and 1938 and at Lichtenburg between 1938 and 1939. The main camp for women, RAVENSBRÜCK, was opened in 1939. The women there, mainly political prisoners, were subject to FORCED LABOR and used in so-called MEDICAL EXPERIMENTS. It is estimated that at any one time, 15 percent of the prisoners there were Jews.

There were over 3,000 uniformed female guards of all ages and occupations working in the Nazi camp system. They were trained in Ravensbrück and then sent to other camps. They learned how to humiliate and exhaust women through work. Some took pleasure in beating and torturing prisoners. Imma Grese, who was considered by the prisoners to be particularly sadistic, worked in Auschwitz and BERGEN-BELSEN.

Johanna Langefeld was a women's camp commandant at Ravensbrück and Auschwitz. Some wives of SS men took part in the terror. For example, Ilse KOCH, the wife of the commandant at BUCHENWALD, had many prisoners killed. After the war, some of these women were convicted at TRIALS OF WAR CRIMINALS.

WORK CAMPS

See LABOR CAMPS.

WORKING GROUP

A Jewish rescue organization active in SLOVAKIA during WORLD WAR II. Some 150,000 JEWS lived in Slovakia (formerly part of CZECHOSLOVAKIA) which the Germans set up as a republic in 1939. The new government

Women at work camp, Auschwitz

was extremely antisemitic and gladly collaborated with the Germans. During 1942, the Jewish community became aware that Jews were about to suffer DEPORTATIONS. Representatives of the Jewish community set up a new organization, the Working Group. It was led by Gisi FLEISCHMANN and Rabbi Michael Ber WEISSMANDEL.

The Working Group first attempted to appeal to church in Slovakia and state authorities. However, the head of state, Josef TISO was a priest, and the church was at the forefront of anti-Jewish activities. The Group then tried buying the safety of the Jews. They held talks with Adolf EICHMANN's representative about paying to save Jewish lives. These talks did not achieve much. The Group also spread bribes throughout the police and other ministries. This did help to rescue a number of individual Jews. Slovakia was paying at the time 500 marks for each Jew deported by the Germans, nominally to cover the cost of new vocational training. The Working Group convinced the authorities that it would be "cheaper" to set up LABOR CAMPS and get those Jews to work. Here again they met with very limited success. The three camps set up—Sered, NOVÁKY, and Vyhne—never housed more than 3,000 persons.

The Working Group undertook several other projects. It sent individuals to find out the fate of Jews deported to POLAND. The Group then sent to the West the first detailed information about AUSCHWITZ, together with a request to bomb this DEATH CAMP. The request was ignored (see AUSCHWITZ BOMBING). The group also succeeded in smuggling some 7,000 Jews into HUNGARY—where they were safe until Germany occupied that country in 1944. In order to finance its activities, the Group first turned to Jewish merchants who had bank accounts abroad. It then appealed to outside Jewish organizations such as the AMERICAN JEWISH JOINT DISTRIBUTION COMMITTEE. The Working Group also helped to finance Jewish armed RESISTANCE in Slovakia.

WORLD JEWISH CONGRESS

(WJC)

Umbrella organization uniting world Jewish communities to speak in one voice in the defense of Jewish rights and to fight rising Nazism. It was founded by Stephen WISE and Nahum Goldmann in 1936. At its founding assembly, the World Jewish Congress (WJC) issued stern warnings about the fate of European Jewry at the hands of the Nazis and called for a boycott of Germany (see BOYCOTTS, ANTI-NAZI) and for the admission of JEWS to PALESTINE and other countries of refuge. In 1940, after the fall of FRANCE, there remained only one WJC outpost on the continent of Europe—in Geneva. WJC action became centered in London—which had also become the seat of exiled governments—and in New York.

In the light of information received from Geneva, the WJC's leadership tried to alert the Allies and neutral churches to the planned destruction of European Jewry. In August 1942, when the RIEGNER CABLE giving information of the "FINAL SOLUTION" reached the WJC offices in London and New York, the reaction of Allied governments informed was at first disbelief and then indifference. The Allied Declaration of 17 December 1942, made simultaneously in London, Washington and Moscow, threatening punishment for the perpetrators of crimes against the Jews, was largely due to WJC efforts.

Among the WJC's successes were:
- intervention with the Bulgarian Church to prevent the deportation of Bulgarian Jewry;
- warning that the Danish Jewry was soon to be deported, which helped in their rescue by Sweden;
- the rescue of over 2,000 children and some 200 adults from FRANCE to SWITZERLAND, SPAIN and Portugal;
- provision of forged papers to several thousand French Jews, enabling them to hide;
- numerous interventions on behalf of Hungarian Jewry, including the unanswered demand to bomb the railway lines leading to AUSCHWITZ to stop the extermination process.

In addition to involvement with the WALLENBERG mission, the Stockholm representative of the WJC was instrumental in the rescue of hundreds of women by Count BERNADOTTE and the Swedish Red Cross from BERGEN-BELSEN early in 1945.

The Atlantic City War Emergency Conference convened by the WJC on 26–30 November 1944, issued a demand for "the fullest measure of justice to the people of Israel." The delegates, representing the Jews of 40 countries, demanded full human and civil rights for the citizens of every country. It also called for abolishing all discriminatory measures against Jews, the rebuilding of destroyed Jewish communities, the capture, trial and punishment of those guilty of crimes against Jews since 1933, payment of reparations for the losses suffered by Jewish communities and individual victims of Nazi crimes, recognition that the Jewish people are entitled to collective reparation for its material and moral losses, and the establishment of Palestine as a Jewish Commonwealth. Practically all these demands were eventually realized.

WORLD WAR II

(1939–1945) The greatest of all armed conflicts in world history. It was the result of the expansionist schemes of the "Axis" powers, GERMANY, JAPAN, and ITALY. Fighting against them were the other major powers of the time: FRANCE, GREAT BRITAIN, and the SOVIET UNION (U.S.S.R.), and later the United States.

The war started on 1 September 1939, when German forces invaded POLAND, defying international commitments. Great Britain and France, which had made promises to defend Poland, declared war on Germany to stop its aggressive policies. However, the Soviet Union, which had previously sought to coordinate its policies with Great Britain and France, made a complete turnabout in August 1939, signing a non-aggression pact with Germany, which included secret clauses for the division of Poland between them (see NAZI-SOVIET PACT). The Germans quickly overran Poland, and then turned their attention to the west. On 9 April 1940, they invaded and soon conquered DENMARK and NORWAY. On 10 May of the same year, their army and air force attacked the NETHERLANDS, BELGIUM, LUXEMBOURG, and France, which quickly fell to them. The Expeditionary Force sent by Great Britain to aid France was driven back. By the end of June 1940, Germany and Italy dominated the continent of Europe from the Atlantic Ocean to the Soviet border.

At this point, the German dictator, Adolf HITLER, hesitated. Initially, he planned to end the war by invading his remaining enemy, Great Britain. However, the Luftwaffe (German Air Force) could not defeat the British Royal Air Force. The Germans then switched from attacking military targets to bombing British cities. Their attempt to end the war by breaking British morale failed.

By the spring of 1941, it looked as if neither

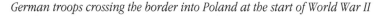

German troops crossing the border into Poland at the start of World War II

Germany nor Britain could defeat the other.

Meanwhile, in September 1940, Italian forces had invaded Egypt, which was occupied by the British, but the Italians were unable to conquer the country. When the British successfully counter-attacked, Hitler sent a force to help the Italians. The war in North Africa was to last until 1943. However, in Hitler's view it was never more than a sideshow.

For ideological as well as strategic reasons, Hitler's interest in the second half of 1940 began shifting to the east. His desire had always been to acquire "living space" (see LEBENSRAUM) for Germany by conquering the Soviet Union. In addition, as long as the Soviet Union remained at his back, he would not be able to triumph over Britain, which was being helped by the United States (in the provision of battleships, for example, although officially the United States was still neutral).

Preparations for "Operation BARBAROSSA," as the German invasion of the Soviet Union was codenamed, went on throughout the winter of 1940–1941 and spring of 1941. By then, Germany had occupied GREECE and YUGOSLAVIA, while the east European countries HUNGARY, ROMANIA, and BULGARIA were allied with them. By June 1941, having concentrated 3.5 million men as well as 2,500 aircraft and 3,500 tanks in the east, the Germans were ready to attack. The invasion of the Soviet Union, which got under way on 22 June to the surprise of the Russian leaders, was the largest single military operation in history.

By December 1941, the German forces, having advanced some 600 miles, were standing at the gates of Moscow. Here they suffered their first serious setback; it is probable that this was the great turning point after which a German victory was no longer possible. The invasion of Russia was also the signal for the implementation of the "FINAL SOLUTION": the large-scale and deliberate murder of European Jewry (the HOLOCAUST).

Meanwhile, the war expanded from Europe to the Far East. Suddenly, on 7 December 1941, the Japanese air force struck at the United States naval base in Pearl Harbor, Hawaii, causing great destruction. A few days later, Hitler declared war on the United States. The war, which had begun as a European conflict, was now truly global. The Japanese overran Southeast Asia and the United States and Japan

Joseph Stalin (left), Harry Truman (center) and Winston Churchill (right) at the Potsdam Conference where the Agreement of Denazification was signed

fought a series of battles in the Pacific.

By June 1942, when the Japanese lost the naval battle of Midway in the Pacific, the tide began to turn. Toward the end of 1942, the Germans reached El Alamein in North Africa and Stalingrad in Russia but were unable to hold onto either and began to retreat on both fronts.

The first region to be cleared of Axis troops was North Africa, in May 1943. This was followed by an Anglo-American invasion of Italy. In September 1943, the Italians surrendered, but the Germans took over northern Italy and were able to hold onto it until April 1945. It was in the vast battles that took place in western Russia in 1943 and 1944 that the most important single source of Axis strength, the German army, was largely destroyed.

In June 1944, American and British forces, who had been building up their strength in England, invaded Normandy in northwestern France (6 June 1944, called D-Day). By the fall of that year, Paris had been liberated and the Allies were standing on Germany's western frontier. However, a combination of supply difficulties and extreme caution on the commanders' part brought the advance to a halt. This enabled Germany to fight on for eight more months. In March, the final Allied offensive was launched on both the eastern and western fronts simultaneously. In April, the Allies, coming from the east and west, met at the Elbe river and brought German resistance to an end. The Germans were surrounded, and 8 May 1945 was celebrated as V-E ("Victory in Europe") Day.

Meanwhile, in the Pacific, Japanese resistance to Allied—primarily American—power was every bit as tough as that of the Germans. Japanese expansion peaked in the summer of 1942, when they controlled a vast perimeter including Korea, most of coastal China, the Philippines, Indochina, Thailand Burma, Malaysia and Singapore, Indonesia and New Guinea, thus threatening Australia. However, Japan's lifelines were slowly cut by the larger, better armed, U.S. Navy. From time to time, there were bitter land battles as American Marines captured Pacific islands, such as Iwo Jima and Okinawa.

By the spring of 1945, American heavy bombers were within range of Japan itself. Tokyo, Japan's capital, was subjected to heavy fire-bombing attacks, which left the city in ruins and perhaps 200,000 of its inhabitants dead. Still, the Japanese would not give up.

Finally, their resistance was broken by two devastating nuclear weapons—atomic bombs—dropped on Hiroshima and Nagasaki on 6 and 9 August with heavy casualties. Two days later, Japan surrendered and V-J ("Victory in Japan") Day was celebrated on 15 August. World War II was over.

YAD LAYELED

see GHETTO FIGHTERS' HOUSE.

YAD VASHEM

Israel's national institution created to enshrine and preserve the memory of the 6 million JEWS murdered and the thousands of European Jewish communities destroyed by Nazi GERMANY. It is a memorial for the study and commemoration of the HOLOCAUST. It is located in Jerusalem on Har ha-Zikaron ("Remembrance Mount").

The idea of a central national project in PALESTINE was already adopted by the first postwar Zionist Conference held in London in August 1945. The name Yad Vashem comes from the biblical Book of

> *"And to them I will give in my house and within my walls a memorial (yad vashem) better than sons and daughters: I will give them an everlasting name, that shall not be cut off."*
>
> *(Isaiah 56:5)*

Isaiah (see box above).

After the State of Israel was established, the Minister of Education and Culture, historian Ben-Zion Dinur, proposed the foundation and the framework for activities of Yad Vashem to the government. In August 1953, representatives of all parties gave their full support to the project and the Martyrs' and Heroes' Remembrance (Yad Vashem) Law was passed.

Yad Vashem, Jerusalem

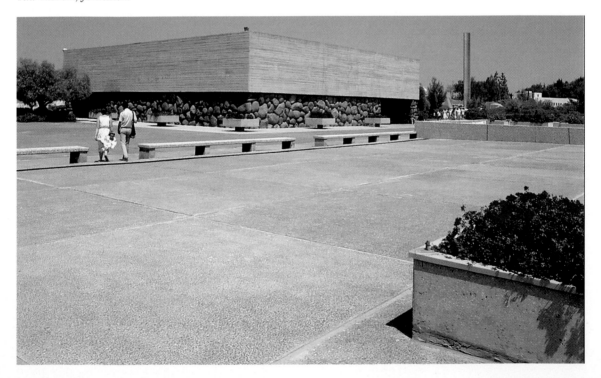

The new institution was intended to commemorate the victims of the Holocaust; the valor and the heroism of Jewish soldiers, the UNDERGROUND and PARTISAN fighters; and the "RIGHTEOUS AMONG THE NATIONS."

The museum's permanent exhibition is arranged chronologically, presenting Adolf HITLER's rise to power, the persecution of the Jews in the THIRD REICH, the destruction by mass murder of Jews by the EINSATZGRUPPEN, the transports to the DEATH CAMPS, Jewish FORCED LABOR, MEDICAL EXPERIMENTS, Jewish armed RESISTANCE and the final stages of the Holocaust.

The Memorial Cave contains hundreds of memorial stones. Participants in the World Gathering of Jewish Holocaust Survivors brought these to Jerusalem with them in 1981. They are engraved with the names of their family and friends murdered in the Holocaust, who have neither grave nor tombstone.

The Hall of Remembrance has a mosaic floor, in which the names of the 22 largest Nazi CONCENTRATION CAMPS are engraved. The central fixture is the Eternal Light, in front of which lies the vault holding the ashes of martyrs, gathered and brought to Israel from the death camps. Commemorative ceremonies are conducted in the Hall, and it is the scene of the state ceremony on HOLOCAUST REMEMBRANCE DAY.

The Valley of the Destroyed Communities commemorates the Jewish communities that were devastated in the Holocaust. The names of some 5,000 ruined communities are engraved there.

In the Children's Memorial Garden is a building which commemorates the one and a half million Jewish CHILDREN who perished in the Holocaust. In its dark interior, five burning memorial candles are multiplied into an infinite number of lights with the use of mirrors, symbolizing the souls of the children whose names are heard being read aloud in the background.

In addition to the memorial halls and sculptures, Yad Vashem has archives and a library that documents the Holocaust in all its aspects. It has published hundreds of books of Holocaust research and recorded tens of thousands of oral TESTIMONIES of Holocaust survivors. Yad Vashem also has a department for the "Righteous Among the Nations," remembering those non-Jews who, for humanitarian reasons, risked their lives to save Jews.

YOM HA-SHOAH

see HOLOCAUST REMEMBRANCE DAY

YOUTH ALIYA

Project of the Zionist movement founded just before Adolf HITLER's rise to power in 1933. It was formed to save Jewish youth from Europe. The project was started in 1932 by Recha Freier, wife of a BERLIN rabbi, who saw the dangers ahead. She arranged for a group of CHILDREN to leave GERMANY to live and be educated in what was then called PALESTINE. In 1933, the Zionist Movement adopted the project and appointed Henrietta Szold (founder of the Hadassah Women's Zionist Organization) to head Youth Aliya ("aliya" is Hebrew for immigration to Palestine/Israel).

By 1935, some 600 young people had been brought from Germany and were living in Palestine on kibbutzim and in agricultural and vocational schools. At that time Hadassah funded the operation. As the Germans spread into AUSTRIA and CZECHOSLOVAKIA the need to save children became more urgent. It was difficult for families to part with their children, but parents realized that by getting them out of Europe they could be saving their lives. By the outbreak of WORLD WAR II, 5,000 children had reached Palestine through Youth Aliya. The British, who were governing the country, would not give immigration certificates for more, so another 15,000 were moved to western European countries, especially GREAT BRITAIN (see KINDERTRANSPORT). Once war broke out, it was almost impossible to get children out of Europe. However, in 1943, a group of 800 children from POLAND who had reached Iran was brought to Palestine (see TEHERAN CHILDREN).

After the war, soldiers of the JEWISH BRIGADE GROUP as well as representatives from Palestine scoured Europe looking for Jewish children and youth who had survived the HOLOCAUST. Some 15,000 were located, most of them orphans. Many had to be smuggled into Palestine in the "illegal" immigration (see ALIYA BET) that was carried out secretly because of strict British limitations on immigration. By then, Youth Aliya had an extensive network of youth villages and educational institutions waiting to receive the children and to look after them.

Members of a Zionist Youth Movement at a training farm in Romania, 1943

YOUTH MOVEMENTS

Jewish youth organizations that arose in Europe between World Wars I and II. They had varying political, religious, and social objectives. Some were Jewish Zionist and prepared members for moving to PALESTINE. Others were communist or socialist. Some, like the Jewish Scouts, had no political character. However, as the turbulent years of the HOLOCAUST unfolded, youth movements and their members across the board rose to the tasks of RESISTANCE and SELF-HELP.

When the Nazis took over eastern Europe, about 100,000 Jewish youth were involved in the various organizations. Early on, the Nazis ordered that they be disbanded. However, rather than disbanding, they maintained their organizations secretly. One such group—The Baum Gruppe—was in Berlin itself. Most of its members were young communists who belonged to Zionist youth movements. They maintained UNDERGROUND activities until 1942. Eventually all were killed.

The effort to keep the organizations active involved great personal risk. Many, like Abba KOVNER, believed that there was no choice. He wrote a declaration to members of the pioneering youth movements in VILNA on 1 January 1942, which said: "Jewish youth, do not be led astray. Hitler aims to destroy all the Jews of Europe. It is better to fall as free fighters than to live by the grace of the murderers. Resist! To the last breath!" Kovner's call to action was heeded by members of the youth movements.

The youth movements played an active role in the resistance. In the WARSAW, VILNA, and other GHETTOS, fighting groups were formed to carry out revolts within the ghetto. In KOVNO, the young activists organized escape into the forests to join with the PARTISANS. Elsewhere, members of the youth movements actively assisted in the rescue and protection of the CHILDREN left behind. In France, for example, 7,000 children whose parents had been deported were taken under protection. Each child was assigned to a member of the UNDERGROUND, who insured his or her physical safety. While many members of the underground teams were caught, nearly all these children survived the war.

The youth movement leaders had a clear understanding of the scope of the Nazi horror. This led them to develop courageous plans to maintain the morale of the Jews—especially the younger generation—under Nazi oppression. They also produced many of the great acts of Jewish resistance.

YOUTH PILGRIMAGES TO HOLOCAUST SITES

Educational trips to Eastern Europe with an emphasis on HOLOCAUST studies. The largest and best-known educational trip is the March of the Living, which first traveled to POLAND in 1988. The name "March of the Living" is derived from the silent walk from AUSCHWITZ I to Auschwitz II-Birkenau that is made by the participants of the pilgrimage. This is an affirmation of life in contrast to the DEATH MARCH, when tens of thousands of Jews were marched from Birkenau, where selections took place, to Auschwitz, where they were murdered in gas chamber #1. After the trip concludes in Poland, the participants travel to Israel for further study.

From 1988 to 1996, approximately 15,000 Jewish youth from 38 countries participated in the silent march. Today, there are many alternative trips to Eastern Europe, with various educational philosophies.

YUGOSLAVIA

Country in southeastern Europe, established in 1918. It was made up of SERBIA, CROATIA, Bosnia and Herzegovina, Macedonia, and other territories. Before WORLD WAR II, there were approximately 80,000 JEWS in Yugoslavia—83 percent of whom perished in

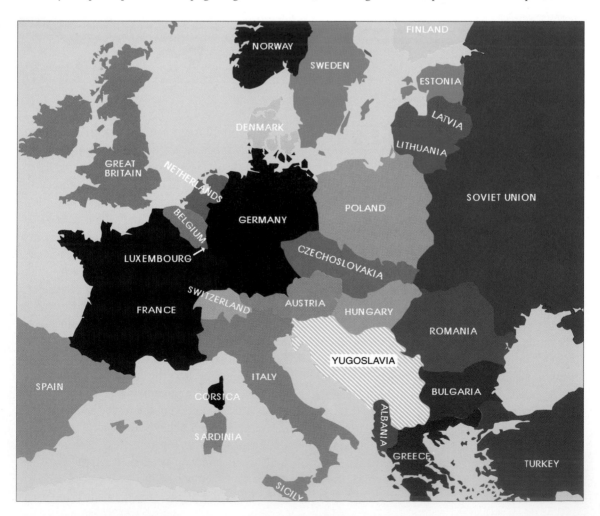

Organizing deportation in Yugoslavia

Gendarmes of the Serbian puppet government lead Gypsies to their execution

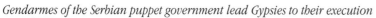

the Holocaust. On 13 April 1941, Nazi GERMANY occupied Yugoslavia and divided the country into five parts. The experiences of Jews varied according to their location.

In German-occupied Serbia, the Germans executed or deported the entire Jewish community. In May 1942, the Germans declared Serbia to be the first area "free of Jews and GYPSIES."

In Croatia, which became an independent state (including Bosnia), the Jews suffered a similar fate. Headed by Ante PAVELIC, the Croatian Jews were forced to register as citizens. Then all of their property and money was taken away. Synagogues and other Jewish institutions were destroyed. The majority of Croatian Jews were later deported to CONCENTRATION CAMPS and by 18 April 1944, it was announced that "Croatia is one of the countries in which the Jewish problem has been solved."

In the Backa region, controlled by Hungary, Jews had to surrender their property and were forced to pay high taxes. Most Jews were sent to FORCED LABOR camps, deported, or murdered. When Germany invaded Hungary in March 1944, the remaining Jews were sent to Germany or to concentration camps. The majority ended up in AUSCHWITZ.

Macedonia was annexed by BULGARIA at the beginning of 1941. Under German pressure, the 7,000 Jews of Macedonia were deported to TREBLINKA DEATH CAMPS in POLAND in 1943 and gassed to death.

Jews fared better in Italian-occupied Yugoslavia. Despite pressure from the Germans, the Italians did not deport the Jews. At the beginning of World War II there were few Jews in this area. However, many more from neighboring parts of Yugoslavia escaped to Italian-occupied areas. The Italians established REFUGEE camps for these Jews. After September 1943, when the PARTISAN army of Tito took control of this area, many Jews joined Tito's revolt. Soon after, in March 1944, the Germans invaded and deported the remaining Jews to the JASENOVAC concentration camp.

In all, some one million Yugoslavians died in World War II. Half of them, including over 60,000 Jews, perished as a result of GENOCIDE.

Z E G O T A

Polish code name for the UNDERGROUND Council for Aid to Jews. It was initiated by a few Poles who were motivated by their Roman Catholic or social democratic values. Zegota provided JEWS with safe hiding places, money, or false identity papers. Participants in Zegota were taking a special risk because in POLAND the penalty for sheltering Jews was death, often of one's family as well.

People participated for different reasons. Some were opposed to the Nazis' murder of the Jews be-

Certificate of Yad Vashem to two leaders of the Zegota Organization naming them "Righteous Among the Nations"

YAD WASHEM
GORA PAMIECI
JEROZOLIMA

יד ושם
הר הזיכרון
ירושלים

תעודה
SWIADECTWO

DZISIAJ, DN. 28. LISTOPADA 1963 ROKU-
NA NASZE ZAPROSZENIE–ZASADZILI DRZEWKA
W ALEI SPRAWIEDLIWYCH NA GÓRZE PAMIĘCI:

Pani Maria Kann
Pan Władysław Bartoszewski

KTÓRZY BYLI CZYNNYMI CZŁONKAMI
RADY "ZEGOTY"
WYŻEJ WYMIENIENI Z NARAŻENIEM
WŁASNEGO ŻYCIA I PODKREŚLENIA
GODNĄ SZLACHETNĄ ODWAGĄ
UCZESTNICZYLI W DZIELE RATOWANIA
PRZEŚLADOWANYCH ŻYDÓW.
IZRAEL NIGDY NIE ZAPOMNI TYCH HUMANITARNYCH CZYNÓW.

cause of their own religious beliefs. Others were tied to Jews by friendships, as classmates or neighbors. Some assisted Jews automatically through acts of human decency. Some of the Poles in Zegota were even known antisemites (SEE ANTISEMITISM), but could not accept the ways in which the Nazis were murdering the Jews.

As Zegota's activities grew, the London-based Polish GOVERNMENT-IN-EXILE recognized its work. However, it was unpopular among much of the general Polish population. Zegota was founded in December 1942 and continued its work until the liberation of Poland in January 1945.

Z O B

see JEWISH FIGHTING ORGANIZATION.

ZUCKERMAN, YITZHAK (A n t e k)

(1915–1981) A leader of the JEWISH FIGHTING ORGANIZATION—ZOB in WARSAW, POLAND during WORLD WAR II. Born in VILNA, LITHUANIA, Zuckerman became a leader of the Dror-He–Haluts Zionist youth movement in 1938 and worked at its headquarters in Warsaw. Soon after the Germans invaded Poland (1 September 1939), Zuckerman fled to Soviet-occupied eastern Poland. There he organized secret Zionist youth groups.

In April 1940, he returned to the German-occupied area to promote Zionist activities there. At this time he met his future wife, and fellow activist Zivia LUBETKIN.

During the DEPORTATIONS from Warsaw in the summer of 1942, Zuckerman called for the use of force against the Germans. As a founder and leader of the ZOB he was sent to KRAKÓW on a mission in December 1942.

He was wounded in the leg and barely managed

Yitzhak Zuckerman (center) at a commemoration in Warsaw, 1945

to get back to Warsaw. On 18 January 1943, Zuckerman led an armed battle with the Germans during a deportation roundup. Just before the WARSAW GHETTO UPRISING began on 19 April 1943, he was ordered to leave the ghetto. Zuckerman was told to represent the ZOB in the rest of Warsaw and to be the liaison with the Polish underground groups. During the uprising he tried to obtain weapons for the rebels and helped to rescue fighters by leading them through the sewers.

When the Polish uprising broke out in Warsaw in August 1944, Zuckerman led a group of Jewish fighters. After the liberation of Poland, Zuckerman and his wife became involved in the BERIHA movement which tried to bring Jews out of eastern Europe and into PALESTINE (Israel). He moved to Palestine in 1947 and was one of the founders of the Ghetto Fighters' Kibbutz and museum, GHETTO FIGHTERS' HOUSE.

ZYGELBOJM, SAMUEL ARTUR

(1895–1943) A leader of the Bund (Jewish Socialist Workers Party) in POLAND, who tried to tell the world what was happening to the JEWS of Europe during the HOLOCAUST.

Zygelbojm, who was born in LUBLIN, settled in WARSAW after World War I, and became active in the Bund. When Warsaw surrendered to the Nazis on 28 September 1939, Zygelbojm was taken hostage by the Germans but was released soon after. Soon after his release—at the risk of his life—he organized an UNDERGROUND cell of the Bund. The Germans set up a JUDENRAT (Jewish Council) in Warsaw in November 1939. Zygelbojm was appointed to it as a Bund representative. Although his Judenrat activities were legal in the eyes of the Germans, his underground Bund activities were not. Fearing arrest, Zygelbojm fled to western Europe at the end of 1939.

From Zygelbojm's farewell letter written before he took his life

I cannot be silent—I cannot live—while remnants of the Jewish people of Poland, of whom I am a representative, are perishing. Responsibility for the murder of the entire Jewish population of Poland lies primarily with the murderers themselves, but indirectly humanity as a whole is responsible, all the Allied nations and their governments who to date have done nothing to stop the crime from going on. I cannot live while the remnants of the Jewish people in Poland are being destroyed. My comrades in the Warsaw ghetto took weapons in their hands on that last heroic impulse. It was not my destiny to die there together with them, but I belong to them, and in their mass graves. By my death I wish to express my strongest protest against the inactivity with which the world is looking on and permitting the extermination of my people.

I know how little human life is worth today; but as I was unable to do anything during my life, perhaps by my death I shall contribute to breaking down the indifference of those who may now—at the last moment—rescue from certain annihilation the few Polish Jews who are still alive. My life belongs to the Jewish people of Poland and I therefore give it to them. I wish that this remaining handful of the original several millions of Polish Jews could live to see the liberation of a new world of freedom, and the justice of true socialism. I believe that such a Poland will arise and that such a world will come.

In September 1940, he escaped to New York, where he continued his activities as Bund representative, warning of the fate of Polish Jewry. In March 1942, he was sent by the Bund to London as its representative to the Polish GOVERNMENT-IN-EXILE. Here he continued trying to inform the Western world of the dangerous situation of the Jews of Europe. In May 1942, he received a detailed report from the Bund in Warsaw on the murder of the Jews in Poland. It listed the sites of DEATH CAMPS and mass shootings. According to the report, approximately 700,000 Jews had already been murdered. Zygelbojm tried to spread this information as widely as possible. He broadcast the news over the British Broadcasting Corporation (BBC) stating, "It will be a disgrace to go on living, to belong to the human race, unless immediate steps are taken to put a stop to this crime, the greatest that history has known."

In September 1942, immediately following the massive DEPORTATION of Jews from the Warsaw GHETTO to TREBLINKA death camp, Zygelbojm announced to the world that 7,000 Jews were being deported from Warsaw every day. Zygelbojm's despair increased, because the Western world was not responding to his pleas. By early 1943, he knew that the end of European Jewry was drawing near.

On 12 May 1943, word came to Zygelbojm about the liquidation of the Warsaw ghetto. Among the last Jews of Warsaw to be killed by the Germans were his wife and 16-year-old son. Responding with a last act of despair, Zygelbojm took his own life. He killed himself, he said in his suicide note, to protest the world's indifference to the fate of the Jews.

Z Y K L O N   B

The trade name of hydrogen cyanide, the deadly poisonous gas used in the DEATH CAMPS of AUSCHWITZ and MAJDANEK.

Zyklon B was manufactured by DEGESCH, German initials for a company that produced pest

Zyklon B pellets and canister as used in the gas chambers of Auschwitz-Birkenau and Majdanek

extermination products, a firm that was controlled by I.G. Farben and the Tesch and Stabenow Company in Hamburg. For ease of delivery, the substance was transported in crystalline form. When used in the GAS CHAMBERS, the crystals were dropped through a resealable hatch. When the crystals came into contact with air, they turned into the deadly gas. Rudolf HÖSS, the commandant of Auschwitz, said that in the tightly sealed gas chambers the victims lost consciousness within a few seconds or minutes. However, death by asphyxiation took at least as long as three to fifteen minutes.

The use of Zyklon B was considered by the Nazis to be an improvement over the crude method of gassing with carbon monoxide, which was used at the BELZEC, SOBIBÓR, TREBLINKA, and CHELMNO death camps. At the postwar trial of the manufacturers of Zyklon B, two of them were condemned to death and executed for supplying the gas in the full knowledge that it was to be used for the murder of death camp inmates. All other defendants were freed by 1951.

chronology

1933

30 January	The Nazi leader Adolf Hitler becomes chancellor of Germany.
20 March	First concentration camp established at Dachau.
1 April	Anti-Jewish boycott in Germany.
10 May	Public burning of books written by Jews and works found offensive to Nazi regime.

1935

15 September	Nuremberg Laws instituted.

1938

13 March	Germany takes over Austria (the Anschluss).
5-15 July	Evian conference fails to solve problem of refugees from Germany.
6 October	Germans take over Sudetenland region of Czechoslovakia.
9-10 November	Kristallnacht pogrom against Jews in Germany and Austria.
12 November	Enormous fine levied on German Jews.

1939

15 March	Germany takes over Czechoslovakia.
May	Refugees aboard the "Saint Louis" refused permission to land in the western hemisphere.
17 May	British issue White Paper severely limiting Jewish immigration to Palestine.
23 August	Germany signs pact with Soviet Russia.

1 September	Germany invades Poland.
3 September	Britain and France declare war on Germany.
28 September	Poland divided between Germany and Soviet Russia.
8 October	Germans establish first ghetto (Piotrków in Poland).
23-28 November	Jews in Generalgouvernement to wear yellow badge and establish Jewish Councils.

1940

9 April	Germany invades Denmark and Norway.
27 April	Orders given to establish camp at Auschwitz.
10 May	Germany invades France, Holland, Belgium, and Luxembourg.
10 June	Italy enters the war on the side of the Germans.
15 June	Soviet Russia occupies Baltic states.
October	Anti-Jewish laws in Vichy France, Netherlands, Bulgaria, and Romania.
15 November	Warsaw Ghetto sealed.

1941

6 April	Germany invades Yugoslavia and Greece.
22 June	Germany invades Russia.
23 June	Einsatzgruppen begin mass killings of Jews in Russia.
July-August	160,000 Jews killed in Bessarabia.
29-30 September	Nearly 34,000 Jews from Kiev killed in Babi Yar.
7 December	Japanese attack U.S. fleet at Pearl Harbor.
10 December	U.S. at war with Germany and Italy
December	Gassing begins in the Chelmno camp.

1942

20 January	Wannsee Conference makes plans for "Final Solution."
17 March	Killings begin in Belzec.
May	Sobibór camp begins operations
22 July	Treblinka camp begins operations.
22 July--12 September	300,000 Jews deported to their deaths from Warsaw Ghetto.
8 November	U.S. and British armies invade North Africa.
11 November	Germans and Italians occupy southern France.
November	Gas chambers begin to operate in Majdanek.

1943

2 February	Battle of Stalingrad ends in Soviet victory.
March	New gas chambers in operation in Auschwitz.
19 April-6 May	Warsaw Ghetto revolt and destruction of the ghetto.
1-2 October	Rescue of Danish Jewry.

1944

19 March	Germans occupy Hungary.
2 May	Hungarian Jews begin to arrive at Auschwitz.
6 June	D Day. U.S. and British forces land in France.
August	France is liberated.

1945

January	Eastern European concentration camps evacuated and prisoners sent on death marches.
27 January	Auschwitz liberated by Soviet army.
March	Jewish Brigade goes into action in northern Italy.
28 April	Mussolini killed by Italian partisans.
30 April	Hitler kills himself; Russian forces take Berlin.
8 May	VE Day. The war in Europe is over.
14 August	Japan surrenders.
18 October	Nuremberg Trials of Nazi leaders begin.

1946

4 July	Pogrom at Kielce, Poland. 100,000 Jewish survivors flee westward.
30 September--1 October	Nuremberg Trial sentences.

1947

July	"Exodus 1947" carrying Holocaust survivors sent back to Germany from Palestine.
29 November	United Nations decides on establishment of a Jewish state.

1948

14 May	State of Israel proclaimed. Welcomes refugees from Displaced Camps in Europe.

an annotated bibliography

Two excellent and comprehensive surveys of the Holocaust are to be found in *The Holocaust* by Leni Yahil (Oxford University Press, 1990, with an extensive and up-to-date bibliography and *The Holocaust* by Nora Levin (Crowell, 1968). (For high school and adult).

Adolf Hitler by Dennis Wepman (Chelsea House, 1989) is a highly readable and well-illustrated biography of Hitler. It discusses how he was able to manipulate adverse economic conditions to his advantage and become Chancellor of Germany. (For junior and senior high school). Another excellent biography is *Hitler* by Albert Marrin (Viking, 1987). It describes his experiences and relationships that shaped his destructive and racist personality. (For junior and senior high school). John Toland's *Adolf Hitler* (Doubleday, 1976) is an excellent analysis of his complex character. It is based on extensive research and interviews with people who knew Hitler. (For high school and adult). *Hitler's Elite* by Louis L. Snyder (Hippocrene Books, 1989) presents a series of short biographies of 19 of Hitler's top staff. (For high school and adult).

One of the most comprehensive histories of Hitler's Germany is *The Rise and Fall of the Third Reich* by William L. Shirer (Simon and Schuster, 1960). It provides a wealth of information that puts the Holocaust into perspective with regard to events occurring in Europe in the 1930s. (For high school and adult). Peter Crisp's *The Rise of Fascism* (Bookwright, 1991) is a well-illustrated history of fascism from its roots in the late 1800s through 1945. It also includes a chronology and glossary. (For high school). *The New Order* (Time-Life Books, 1989) is an excellent photographic presentation of 1930s Germany. (For high school). *The Origins of Nazi Genocide* by Henry Friedlander (University of North Carolina Press, 1995) is based on extensive research and details the Nazi program of exterminating the handicapped and disabled. This program eventually evolved into the systematic destruction of Jews and Gypsies. (For high school and adult). Arno J. Mayer's *Why Did the Heavens Not Darken?* (Pantheon, 1989) is an interesting study that claims the destruction of Jews was not part of the original plan, but was developed when the German campaign against the U.S.S.R. failed during World War II. (For high school). *Atlas of Nazi Germany* edited by Michael Freeman and Tim Mason (Macmillan, 1987) is an excellent general atlas showing the location of the concentration camps and death camps. (For Junior and senior high school). An essential resource is the *Encyclopedia of the Third Reich* (Macmillan, 1991, 2 vols). It contains well written articles on all aspects of Nazi Germany. (For high school and adult).

Life in the Third Reich edited by Richard Bessel (Oxford University Press, 1987) is a collection of eight essays by leading historians. (For high school and adult). Bernt Engelmann's *In Hitler's Germany* (Pantheon Book, 1986) is based on interviews of supporters of Hitler and those who opposed him in an attempt to see beyond generalizations to the reality of life under Hitler. (For high school and adult). Peter Neville's *Life in the Third Reich: World War II* (Batsford, 1992) is an insightful narrative that examines the causes, events, and outcome of the rise of the Nazi party in 1933. (For junior and senior high school). Johannes Steinhoff's *Voices from the Third Reich* (Da Capo, 1994) presents a grim picture of life in Germany through the personal stories of more than 150 concentration camp survivors, SS men, resistance activists, and teenage Nazis. (For high school and adult). *Children of the Swastika: The Hitler Youth* by Ellen Heyes (Millbrook, 1993) puts the reality of fascism into perspective with the story of the Hitler Youth movement. (For junior and senior high school). Another vivid account of growing up in Nazi Germany is Ilse Koehn's *Mischling, Second Degree: My Childhood in Nazi Germany* (Greenwillow, 1977). It is the story of a young girl's experiences in a paramilitary girl's camp in occupied territory. Her parents did not tell her she was part Jewish. (For junior and senior high school).*Cities at War, Berlin* by Eleanor H. Ayer (New Discovery Books, 1992) examines the effects of World War II on the people of Berlin. (For junior high school).

The Architect of Genocide: Himmler and the Final Solution by Richard Breitman (Knopf, 1991) is an excellent biography of the head of the SS. He created the plans and schemes that eventually led to the killing of 6 million Jews and other groups whom the Nazis called "undesirable". (For high school and adult). *The War Against the Jews 1933–1945* by Lucy S. Dawidowicz (Holt, 1975) is an excellent comprehensive history of Nazi destruction of European Jews. It focuses on the ideology and procedures that allowed the state to murder entire segments of its population. (For high school and adult). *The Yellow Star: The Persecution of the Jews in Europe, 1933–45* by Gerhard Schoenberner (Bantam Books, 1979) is a well illustrated overview of the Holocaust with brief summaries of the events. (For junior and senior high school). Rita Thalmann and Emmanuel Feinermann's *Crystal Night 9–10 November, 1938* (Putnam, 1974) is based on contemporary documents and tells the story of the night that terrorized Jews in Nazi Germany. Hundreds of Jews were killed and thousands of Jewish businesses and synagogues were destroyed. (For junior high school). *The Ninth of November* by Hannele Zurndorfer (Quartet Books, 1983) is the story of two sisters in 1930's Germany and the events of *Kristallnacht*. (For junior and senior high school).

The Historical Atlas of the Holocaust (Macmillan, 1995, also available on CD-ROM) is a superb reference tool. It was designed and created by the United States Holocaust Memorial Museum, and contains over 200 full color maps, providing the locations of the camps and ghettos. It also shows the borders of the European countries as they changed from 1933 to 1945. (For high school and adult). Martin Gilbert's *The Holocaust: Maps and Photographs* (Hill and Wang, 1987) provides comprehensive, well illustrated summaries of the events and their locations. (For high school). *Encyclopedia of the Holocaust* (Macmillan, 1990, 4 vols). is very comprehensive, containing over 1,000 well balanced articles on all aspects of the Holocaust.

Miriam Chaikin's *A Nightmare in History: The Holocaust, 1933–1945* (Clarion Books, 1987) is a well illustrated readable account of the development of antisemitism, the rise of Hitler, the Warsaw Ghetto uprising, and the death camps. (For junior high school).

The Holocaust: The Fire that Raged by Seymour Rossel (Watts, 1989) presents a concise chronicle of events beginning with the Treaty of Versailles through the Nuremberg Trials highlighting key political decisions that enabled the Nazi Party to rise to power. (For junior high school). *Never to Forget* by Milton Meltzer (Harper/Trophy 1991) is a well written human history of the Nazi extermination of the Jews. (For junior and senior high school). *Tell Them We Remember: The Story of the Holocaust* by Susan D. Bachrach (Little, Brown, 1994) is a well illustrated account of the lives of 20 people caught up in Germany. An excellent chronology from 1933 to 1948 when Israel became an independent country is also included. (For high school). Yitzhak Arad's *The Pictorial History of the Holocaust* (Macmillan, 1992) contains over 400 photos and maps. The text and photos provide a vivid chronicle of the Nazis, "final solution." (For junior and senior high school). Gerda Haas' *Tracking the Holocaust* (Runestone Press, 1995) is an excellent chronology of the events in Europe from 1930 to 1950. It tells eight stories of survival, including the author's, to illustrate the effects of the Holocaust. (For high school). An outstanding introduction is Ronnie Landau's *The Nazi Holocaust* (Ivan Dee, 1994). It covers the moral and psychological questions raised by the Holocaust as well as the historical events. (For high school and adult). Martin Gilbert's *The Holocaust: The History of Jews of Europe During the Second World War* (Holt 1986) is based on records and testimony of survivors and provides a chronological overview of the attempt to annihilate the Jews of Europe. (For high school and adult). *The Holocaust and the Crisis of Human Behavior* by George M. Kren and Leon Rappoport (Holmes and Meier, Rev. ed., 1994) is an excellent analysis of the factors contributing to the Holocaust and its effect on the perpetrators, victims, bystanders, and resisters. (For high school and adult). David S. Wyman's *The Abandonment of the Jews: America and the Holocaust 1941–1945* (Pantheon, 1984) is a well researched book documenting the response of the United States to the events in Europe. The roles of Congress and the President during the war and the effect of the U.S. immigration quotas are also discussed. (For high school and adult).

We Remember the Holocaust by David A. Adler (Holt, 1995) is an excellent introduction to the history of the Holocaust and is based on personal interviews with many survivors and their families. It includes photographs, a chronology, and a glossary. (For junior and senior high school). *Smoke and Ashes* by Barbara Rogasky (Holiday, 1988) is a detailed history combining eyewitness accounts with graphic photographs many of which were taken by Nazis. (For junior high school). Lila Perl and Marion Blumenthal Lazar's *Four Perfect Pebbles* (Greenwillow Books, 1996) is the personal story of a family's life in Germany, Holland, prison camp, liberation, and their three year struggle to emigrate to the United States. (For junior and senior high school). Laurel Holliday's *Children in the Holocaust and World War II* (Pocket Books, 1995) is an anthology of diaries written by children in Nazi occupied Europe. Not all of the 22 children survived the horrors of daily life. (For junior and senior high school). *Escape or Die* by Ina R. Friedman (Harper, 1982) is a recounting of the stories of survival of 12 men and women who escaped Hitler's final solution. (For high school). *Holocaust Testimonies* by Lawrence L. Langer (Yale University Press, 1993) analyzes how oral testimony of survivor complements historical research in the telling of history. (For high school and adult). *A Holocaust Reader* edited by Lucy S. Dawidowicz (Behrman, 1976) is a collection of official records and private papers dealing with Nazi persecution and destruction of the Jews. (For high school and adult).

Witness to the Holocaust:An Oral History edited by Rhonda G. Lewin (Twayne, 1990) is a well organized presentation of the stories of 21 men, women, and children who survived the camps; 23 people who hid, fled, or fought with the Resistance: and 14 Americans who entered the camps as liberators. *Witness to the Holocaust* edited by Azriel Eisenberg is an impressive anthology of eye-witness accounts covering all aspects of the Holocaust (Pilgrim Press, 1981). (For high school and adult).

Gerda Haas' *These I Do Remember: Fragments from the Holocaust* (Cumberland, 1982) provides a geographically diverse view of the Holocaust through excerpts from letters, diaries, and eyewitness accounts. (For high school). Howard Greenfeld's *The Hidden Children* (Ticknor & Fields, 1993) presents the stories of 13 men and women who, as children, were hidden from the Nazis by strangers, in convents, or in orphanages. (For junior and senior high school). *Different Voices: Women and the Holocaust* edited by Carol Rittner and John K. Roth (Paragon House, 1993) is based on the written memoirs, letters, and poetry of 28 women, provides a history of women in the Holocaust, includes maps, photos, chronology and glossary. (For high school and adult). *Playing for Time* by Fania Fenelon and Marcelle Routier (Atheneum, 1977) is the story of the author's survival of Birkenau by playing in the camp's orchestra for the SS guards. (For high school and adult). *Women of Theresienstadt* edited by Ruth Schwertfeger (St. Martins, 1989) tells the story of 20 women inmates from the female perspective. Many of the finest European Jewish musicians were interned at Theresienstadt. (For high school and adult). Ina R. Friedman's *The Other Victims* (Houghton Mifflin, 1990) presents the equally compelling stories of the victimized gentiles: gypsies, homosexuals, Jehovah's Witnesses, political dissenters, disabled, etc. (For high school and adult).

There are many different editions of the *Diary of Anne Frank* for every age level. *The Diary of Anne Frank: The Critical Edition* (Doubleday, 1989) adds commentary and analysis of the Frank family life in Amsterdam to the diary she kept during two years in hiding. (For junior and senior high school). Ruud van der Rol and Rian Verhoeven's *Anne Frank: Beyond the Diary* (Viking, 1993) describes Anne Frank's life before the family went into hiding, illustrated with many photographs taken by her father. (For junior and senior high school). *The Last Seven Months of Anne Frank* by Willy Lindwer (Pantheon, 1991) is a reconstruction of her life in the Bergen-Belsen concentration camp from reminiscences of the survivors who knew her. (For junior and senior high school). *Anne Frank Remembered* by Miep Gies and Alison Leslie Gold (Simon and Schuster, 1987) adds perspective to the story of Anne Frank. The author helped hide the Frank family from the Nazis. (For high school and adult). Another story of hiding is *The Upstairs Room* by Johanna Reiss (Harper/Crowell, 1972). It is based on the experiences of the author and her sister during World War II. (For junior high school). Also by Johanna Reiss is *The Journey Back* (Crowell, 1976) the sequel to *The Upstairs Room* and tells of the end of the war and their family's liberation from hiding. (For junior high school). *Elie Wiesel: Witness for Life* by Ellen Norman Stern (Ktav Publishing House, 1982) is a good biography of one of the more famous survivors of the camps. (For junior high school). Elie Wiesel's *The Night Trilogy: Night, Dawn, The Accident* (Hill & Wang, 1987) is a stark autobiographical account of life in Buchenwald concentration camp where he watched his father die. (For high school and adult). Another personal memoir by Elie Weisel is *Legends of Our Time* (Holt, 1968). (For high school and adult). *Surviving and Other Essays* by Bruno Bettelheim (Knopf, 1979) is a series of essays by Bettelheim. They confront the psychological and philosophical issues of the evil of the Holocaust and survival. (For high school and adult).

In The Camps by Erich Hartmann (Norton, 1995) tells the story of Dachau through photographs of the camp as it appears today. (For high school and adult). Another photographic study presents the camps as they appear today is *Deathly Still: Pictures of Concentration Camps* by Dirk Reinartz (Art Publishers, 1995). (For high school and adult). Diana Dewar's *Saint of Auschwitz: The Story of Maximilian Kolbe* (Harper, 1983) is the story of a Polish Franciscan priest who gave his life for a fellow prisoner. Maximilian Kolbe was canonized as a Catholic saint in 1982. (For high school and adult). *Auschwitz: A History in Photographs* edited by Teresa Swiebocka (Indiana University Press, 1993) is a comprehensive photographic record of Auschwitz during the Holocaust and today. (For high school and adult). *Smoke Over Birkenau* by Liana Millu (Jewish Publication Society, 1991) tells the stories of the women prisoners of Birkenau. Both the violence and tragedy, but also friendship and endurance. (For high school).

The Buchenwald Report edited by David A. Hackett (Westview, 1995) represents the only systematic interviewing of prisoners about daily life and camp structure by the liberating U.S. Army. (For high school and adult). Joe Hyams' *A Field of Buttercups* (Prentice-Hall, 1968) is the story of Dr. Janusz Korczak and his experiences in the Warsaw ghetto with the children of his orphanage. (For junior high school). *Father of the Orphans* by Mark Bernheim (Dutton, 1989) is another very good biography of Dr. Janusz Korczak. He defied the Nazis and refused to turn over the children in his orphanage. He died with them in Treblinka death camp. (For junior high school). *Treblinka* by Jean Francis Steiner (Simon and Schuster, 1967) recounts the story of the 600 Jews who revolted against the Nazis and burned the camp to the ground. (For high school and adult).

Roman Vishniac's A *Vanished World* (Farrar, Straus, 1983) is a photographic documentary of Jewish life in Poland before the beginning of World War II. (For high school).*A Cup of Tears: A Diary of the Warsaw Ghetto* by Abraham Lewin, (Basil Blackwell, 1989) is the diary of a Jewish teacher. It tells of life and death and the ominous presence of the Nazis in Warsaw. (For high school and adult). *In the Warsaw Ghetto, Summer 1941* by Willy Georg (Aperture Foundation, 1993) includes comments from diaries of people trapped in the Warsaw ghetto. Some of the photographs were secretly taken by German soldiers. (For junior and senior high school). *The Warsaw Ghetto in Photographs* edited by Ulrich Keller (Dover, 1984) is a collection of photographs taken by the German Army in 1941 to document conditions in the ghetto. (For junior and senior high school). Two recently published books on the uprising are: Karen Zeinert's *The Warsaw Ghetto Uprising* (Millbrook, 1993) which provides an excellent account of the 28 day struggle in Warsaw. It contains a chronology of events. (For junior and senior high school). Also entitled *The Warsaw Ghetto Uprising* by Elaine Landau (Macmillan, 1992) presents the story of the struggle of the Jewish underground during April and May, 1943. (For junior and senior high school). *Do Not Go Gentle: A Memoir of*

Jewish Resistance in Poland, 1941–1945 by Charles Gelman (Archon Books, 1989) tells of the personal experiences of a boy who joined the partisans as a teenager in Nazi occupied Poland. (For junior and senior high school). Three books by Ruth Minsky Sender tell her life story from the ghetto at Lódz, Poland, through the concentration camps; to liberation and the search for family and the eventual emigration to the United States; and finally, she describes the impact of the Holocaust on her, and of her attempts to teach children about her experiences. The titles are: *The Cage* (Macmillan, 1986,), *To Life* (Macmillan, 1988), and *The Holocaust Lady* (Macmillan, 1992). (All are for junior high school).

The Big Lie: A True Story by Isabella Leitner (Scholastic, 1992) tells of the experiences of the author and her family after the Nazi invasion of Hungary. Their internment at Auschwitz where her mother and baby sister were gassed. And, eventually, they were reunited with their father in the United States. (For junior high school). *In Young People Speak, Surviving the Holocaust in Hungary* edited by Andrew Handler and Susan Meschel (Watts, 1993) eleven survivors tell of their childhood experiences in Nazi occupied Hungary. (For junior high school).

Cities at War, Amsterdam by Victoria Sherrow (New Discovery Books, 1992) is a good general history, including some eyewitness observations, of the German occupation of Amsterdam from 1940 to its liberation in 1945. (For junior high school). Clara Asscher-Pinkoff's *Star Children* (Wayne State University Press, 1986) tells the story of the children in the Amsterdam ghetto and how they contended with daily life in the ghetto and concentration camps. (For junior high school). *The Hiding Place* by Carrie Ten Boom (Bantam Books, 1983) presents the story of a non-Jewish heroine of the Dutch underground who was caught and sent to Ravensbrück concentration camp for hiding Jews. (For junior high school).

Yehuda Bauer's *They Chose Life, Jewish Resistance in the Holocaust* (American Jewish Committee, 1973) provides a good overview of the Jewish underground and resistance movements during the Holocaust. (For junior high school). Lore Cowan's *Children of Resistance* (Meredith Press, 1969) relates the true stories of young people who fought the Nazis. (For junior high school). *Against All Hope: Resistance in the Nazi Concentration Camps* by Hermann Langbein (Paragon House, 1994) documents a wide range of organized overt acts of rebellion and sabotage by Jews within the camps. (For high school and adult). *In Kindling Flame: The Story of Hannah Senesh, 1921–1944* by Linda Atkinson (Lothrop, 1984) is the well written biography of a young Jewish fighter from Palestine who was captured after parachuting into Nazi occupied territory. (For high school).

Rescuers by Gay Block and Malka Drucker (Holmes and Meier, 1992) tells the stories of 49 people from ten different countries who risked their lives and the lives of their families to hide Jews, obtain false papers, and smuggle people out of ghettos. (For junior high school). Carol Rittner's *The Courage to Care* (New York University Press, 1986) profiles a number of Gentiles who saved many Jews from the camps. (For junior and senior high school). Milton Meltzer's *Rescue: The Story of How Gentiles Saved Jews in the Holocaust* (Harpercollins Juvenile Books, 1988) tells the personal stories of many men, women, priests, nuns, and whole villages who worked to save as many Jews as they could. (For junior and senior high school). *Shattering the German Night: The Story of the White Rose* by Annette Dumbach (Little, Brown, 1986) is the story of young Germans and their resistance organization and their work against the Nazi movement. (For high school and adult). *The White Rose* by Inge Scholl (Wesleyan University Press, 1983) tells of the personal involvement of the author's family in the German underground, their work against the Nazi government, and their deaths. (For high school and adult). John Bierman's *Righteous Gentile: The Story of Raoul Wallenberg* (Viking, 1981) is a well done account of the Swedish diplomat's efforts to save thousands of Hungarian Jews. He disappeared in 1945. (For junior and senior high school). *Raoul Wallenberg* by Harvey Rosenfeld (Holmes & Meier, 1995) is an excellent biography of the Swedish diplomat who saved 100,000 Hungarian Jews. (For high school and adult). Thomas Keneally's *Schindler's List* (Simon & Schuster, 1982) is a powerful novel about a German business owner who shielded his Jewish workers in Poland from the Nazis. (For high school and adult). *Secret Ship* by Ruth Kluger and Peggy Mann (Doubleday, 1978) presents the tremendous obstacles faced by the Jews who fled the Nazis on the ship *Hilda* for Palestine. (For junior high school). *Kindertransport* by Olga Levy Drucker (Holt, 1992) tells of the evacuation of many German Jewish children to England and their experiences in England during World War II. (For junior high school).

Target Hitler: The Plots to Kill Adolf Hitler by James P. Duffy and Vincent L. Ricci (Praeger, 1992) recounts the many attempts beginning in 1938 on Hitler's life. This narrative concentrates on the group of conspirators within the German army and culminates in the July 1944 attempted assassination by bombing his headquarters. (For high school and adult). *An Honorable Defeat* by Anton Gill (Holt, 1994) is based on archival material and interviews with the few resisters and family members who survived detection. All risked death, especially the army officers, Foreign Service, and Abwehr for their few achievements. (For high school and adult). Ada Petrova and Peter Watson's *The Death of Hitler* (Norton, 1995) is a well written narrative based on the material found in the Russian archives that deals with the physical evidence of Hitler's death in Berlin, 1945. Information relating to the death of Goebbels and his family is also included. (For high school and adult).

Elaine Landau's *Nazi War Criminals* (Watts, 1990) is a well documented account of Nazi war criminals who went into hiding, and eventually, those who found them. (For junior and senior high school). Robert E. Conot's *Justice at Nuremberg* (Harper, 1983) is an excellent analysis of the trials of the Nazi war criminals. It includes portraits of the people involved and insight into the complex legal proceedings. (For high school and adult). *Long Knives and Short Memories* by Jack Fishman (Richardson and Steirman, 1986) is more the story of the prison than of the seven men who were sentenced to serve time at Spandau Prison. (For high school and adult). *Justice in Jerusalem* by Gideon Hausner (Harper and Row, 1966) is a well written account of Eichmann's trial in Israel. Hausner led the prosecution at the trial. (For high school and adult). Erhardt Dabringhaus' *Klaus Barbie* (Acropolis, 1984) describes the United States involvement and use of Barbie as an agent to supply information on communist activities. Barbie was called the Butcher of Lyon and was responsible for 4,000 murders and 8,000 deportations. (For high school and adult). Simon Wiesenthal's *The Sunflower* (Schocken, 1976) is the autobiography of the famed Nazi hunter. It is well written and provides a great deal of insight into the man and his mission. (For high school and adult). Albert Speer, Hitler's architect and minister of armaments, wrote his memoirs *Inside the Third Reich* (Macmillan, 1970), (For high school and adult).

The Aftermath: Living With the Holocaust by Aaron Hass (Cambridge University Press, 1995) deals with the children of survivors and their attempts to reconstruct their heritage and understanding what their parents went through. (For high school and adult). Yale Strom's *A Tree Still Stands: Jewish Youth in Eastern Europe Today* (Philomel, 1990) is a series of photo essays about how contemporary Jewish teenagers in Eastern Europe are living today. All are descendants of survivors of the Holocaust. (For high school). *Schindler's Legacy: True Stories of the List Survivors* by Elinor Brecher (Hodder & Stoughton, 1994) provides insight into the lives of the people assisted by Schindler. (For high school and adult). *Can It Happen Again?* edited by Roselle Chartock and Jack Spencer (Black Dog and Leventhal, 1995) is a collection of over 100 articles by eyewitnesses and survivors. Recent articles discuss the oppression and genocide in Europe, Africa, Asia, and the Americas. (For high school and adult). *Denying the Holocaust* by Deborah Lipstadt (Free Press, 1993) presents a full account of the revisionist movement challenging the existence of the Holocaust. (For high school and adult). *The Good Old Days: The Holocaust as Seen by Its Perpetrators and Bystanders* edited by Ernst Klee, Willi Dressen and Volker Riess (Free Press, 1991) compiles diary and journal entries, interviews and photographs from the photo album of the Commandant of Treblinka into an interesting report. Taken together, these documents challenge the argument that the people who carried out the Holocaust were just following orders. (For high school and adult).

The World Must Know by Michael Berenbaum (Little, Brown, 1993) is the story of the Holocaust through the collection at the United States Holocaust Memorial Museum in Washington D.C. It includes a thorough chronicle of events illustrated with many archival photographs. (For junior and senior high school). Jeshajahu Weinberg and Rina Elieli's *The Holocaust Museum in Washington* (Rizzoli, 1995) is the story of the museum, itself. How it was planned, constructed, and designed to create a meaningful experience for the visitors. (For junior and senior high school). *The United States Holocaust Memorial Museum* by Eleanor H. Ayer (Silver Burdett Press, 1995) takes the reader on a floor by floor tour of the museum and its exhibits. It also provides an overview of Holocaust historiography from 1933 to the present. (For junior high school).

There are many different video tapes available on any aspect of the Holocaust for every age level. Some of the best are for classroom use as history lessons. Some are theatrical movies and as such, maybe fictionalized history. The videos listed below are just a sampling of what is available. *Mein Kampf* (Columbia, 1961) is a comprehensive documentary of Hitler's rise to power. It includes archival photos and newsreel footage. (For high school and adult). *A New Germany 1933–1939* (Thames Television) is part 1 of the *World at War* series. It is an award winning presentation of early Nazi history. (For high school and adult). *Heil Hitler: Confessions of a Hitler Youth* (HBO, 1991) utilizes graphic documentary footage to dramatize how youth camps, speeches and education were used to re-enforce Hitler's message. (For junior and senior high school). *Geno-cide (*Thames Television) is part 20 of the *World at War* series. It documents the methods employed by the Nazis to exterminate Jews and other undesirable groups. Also included are interviews with survivors. (For high school and adult). *More Than Broken Glass: Memories of Kristallnacht* (ERGO) places the events of Kristallnacht into historical perspective of 1930's Germany. (For junior and senior high school). *Night and Fog (Nuit et Brouillard)* is an excellent French film. This short documentary effectively combines actual black and white footage of concentration camps with color film of the same areas 10 years later. (For high school and adult). *The Struggles for Poland* (PBS) presents excellent newsreel documentation of the Nazis systematic anni-hilation of Polish Jews. (For high school and adult). *Heritage: Civilization and the Jews—Out of the Ashes* (Films, Inc). is narrated by Abba Eban and it examines the Holo-caust as a universal tragedy. (For high school and adult). *The Last Nazi* (Coronet/MTI Film & Video) is an interview from Spandau Prison with Albert Speer. He reflects on his life, attitudes, and the events he helped to create. (For high school and adult). *America and the Holocaust* (WGBH) is a well researched documentary that tells the story of the restrictive immigration policy of the United States during World War II. This policy prevented hundreds of thousands of Jews from emigrating to the United States. (For high school and adult).

Four excellent movies that approach the Holocaust from different perspectives are *The Diary of Anne Frank, Schindler's List, Shoah,* and *Judgment at Nuremberg.* All four are available on video. (For high school and adult).

cumulative index

Darkened numbers indicate an entry on the subject

186, 196, 216, 231,
233, 241, 270, 284,
287, 291, 303, 316,
317, 322, 323, 338,
343, 366, 392, 419,
429, 432, 439, 441
Bermuda 408
Bernadotte, Count
Folke **54**, 379, 435
Bessarabia 26, **55-56**,
93, 278, 335, 336,
371, 373, 393, 394,
416
Best, Werner **56**, 99,
110
Biala Waka 164
Bialystok 44, 45, **56-57**,
162, 328, 350, 374,
387, 388, 395, 396
Bieberstein, Dr. Marek
227
Biebow, Hans **57**
Bielski, Tuvia, Zusya,
Asael, and Aharon
57-58, 131, 299

Bikernietzi forest
233
Bilgoraj 214
Birkenau 20, 35, 37, 73,
92, 104, 153, 190,
195, 210, 228, 271,
272, 328, 371, 442
Bizerte 401
Blobel, Paul 13, 14, **58**
Bloom, Hyman 32
Blum, Léon **58-59**, 262
Bohemia 43, **59-60**, 88,
112, 180, 196, 241,
283, 284, 311, 355,
389, 390
Bohne, Josef 242
Bolivia 28, 46, 233, 335
Bonhoeffer, Dietrich
60, 79
Bordeaux 359
Borki 14
Bormann, Martin **61-
62**, 288
Born, Friedrich 319
Borowski, Tadeusz **62**

Bosnia-Herzegovina
300, 442, 444
Bosshammer, Friedrich
338
Bouhler, Philipp 123
Bousquet, René **62**
Bradley, General 119
Brand, Hansi 64
Brand, Joel Jenö **64**
Brandenburg 123
Brandt, Karl **64**, 123,
124
Braslav, Shmuel 209
Bratislava 65, 123, 138,
295, 433
Brazil 232, 233, 264,
265, 369, 396
Britain (see Great
Britain)
Brú Federico Laredo
344
Brundage, Avery 292
Brunner, Alois **65**, 109,
172, 345, 346, 415
Brussels 47, 48, 103,

134
Brzezinka 195
Buber, Martin 159, 192
Bucharest **65-66**, 200,
376
Buchenwald 31, 37, 59,
66-67, 82, 95, 107,
141, 146, 153, 176,
210, 222, 229, 243,
430, 434
Budapest 29, 64, **67-
69**, 93, 163, 197,
217, 250, 295, 300,
319, 323, 324, 333,
366, 381, 417, 418
Buege, Emil 104
Buenos Aires 28
Bukbuk 240
Bukovina 26, 55, **69**,
93, 335, 336, 373,
393, 402, 416
Bulgaria 43, **69-71**, 139,
171, 183, 196, 297,
336, 411, 437, 444
Buna-Monowitz 38, 83,

92, 199, 237
Burckhardt, Dr. Carl J.
330
Buresova, Charlotte 29
Burma 438
Burns, Eva Gerstl 94
Byelorussia 42, 57, **71**,
81, 93, 117, 131,
154, 265, 293, 297,
376
Bytom 220, 353

C
Cairo 64, 198
Calarasi 206
Cambodia 193
Canada 54, **74**, 110,
141, 170, 193, 280,
360, 379, 412
Canaris, Admiral Wil-
helm 13, **74-75**,
Caribbean 18, 180
Carol, King of Romania
26, 167, 200
Carter, President Jimmy

271, 410, 430
Ceaucescu, President
Nicholae 395
Celan, Paul 244
Chagall, Marc 33, 148
Chamberlain, Houston
Stewart 316
Chamberlain, Neville
26, 27, 80, 344
Chaplin, Charles 135,
136
Charleroi 48
Chelmno (Kulmhof) 57,
75-76, 92, 151, 153,
176, 216, 247, 308,
341, 424, 448
Chile 232, 233
China, 204, 205, 352,
438
Chirac, Jacques 144,
414
Chomsky, Marvin 135
Christian X, King 99
Christianstadt 94
Christopher, Warren

148, 149

Churchill, Winston
Leonard Spencer 26,
80, 170, 184, 191,
299, 397, 406, 432,
437

Clauberg, Dr.Carl 263,
318, 371

Cluj 200, 395

Coburg 342

Codreanu, Corneliu
Zelea 200

Cohen, Arthur A. 192

Cohen, David 282

Cologne 158

Constanta 52, 337, 372

Copenhagen 110

Corfu 173

Coughlin, Father
Charles 18

Coward, Charles **83**

Crete 171

Crimea 117

Croatia **84**, 133, 147,
198, 205, 299, 300,

411, 442, 444

Cuba 232, 344

Curaçao 376

Cusa, Alexandru C. 200

Cyprus 17, 52, **84-85**,
106, 294

Czechoslovakia 27, 59,
64, 77, **85-88**, 101,
108, 112, 116, 160,
185, 188, 189, 241,
303, 310, 320, 323,
341, 347, 355, 358,
389, 392, 393, 397,
440

Czerniaków, Adam **88**,
103, 214, 216, 222,
420, 421

Czernowitz (Cernauti,
Chernovtsy) 69

Czestochowa 162

D

Dachau 33, 37, 59, 62,
82, **89-90**, 93, 94,
95, 116, 141, 146,

176, 181, 195, 226,
228, 229, 239, 241,
262, 263, 277, 283

Dalvege, Kurt 59

Damaskinos,
Archbishop
Theophilus 172, 173

Damascus 65, 198

Dannecker, Theodor
15, 70, 203, 338

Danzig (Gdánsk) **90-
91**, 95, 218, 235,
243, 374

Darlan, Admiral 15

Darquier de Pellepoix,
Louis **91**, 143, 413

Darré, Richard Walter
91

Daruvar 147

Daugavpils (Dvinsk)
233

Davod 147

Dawidowicz, Lucy 184,
188

Dawidson, Gusta (see

205, 211, 212, 215, 219, 226, 228, 230, 232, 236, 238, 243, 263, 264, 268, 270, 271, 274, 275, 277, 278, 279, 280, 281, 282, 283, 284, 290, 291, 292, 302, 303, 304, 310, 313, 314, 315, 321, 322, 323, 328, 334, 336, 339, 340, 342, 343, 347, 351, 355, 361, 366, 367, 369, 373, 376, 377, 381, 392, 412, 419, 424, 426, 427, 436, 437, 439, 440

Hlinka, Andrej 187

Hochhuth, Rolf 243

Hohensalza 424

Holland (see Netherlands, the)

Holland, Agnieszka 135, 136

Holliday, L. 103

Horthy, Miklós 29, 69, **194-195**, 196, 197, 328, 381

Höss, Rudolf 37, 176, **195-196**, 399, 448

Huber, Kurt 429, 430

Hull, Cordell 398

Hungary 25, 29, 35, 43, 64, 67, 81, 86, 103, 133, 138, 139, 163, 173, 176, 183, 190, 194, 195, **196-198**, 217, 250, 295, 303, 319, 323, 324, 325, 328, 333, 336, 354, 355, 371, 381, 390, 395, 399, 417, 432, 435, 437, 444

Hunsche, Otto 64

Husseini, Hajj Amin al **198**

I

Ile d'Yeu 301

India 377

Indochina 438

Indonesia 438

Iran 387, 440

Iraq 198, **200**

Isle of Man 170

Israel, State of 25, 28, 31, 33, 49, 69, 71, 85, 106, 114, 115, 125, 163, 171, 191, 192, 193, **200-201**, 211, 227, 239, 244, 271, 294, 296, 309, 320, 324, 325, 357, 369, 371, 376, 377, 379, 381, 396, 399, 400, 409, 410, 426, 437, 442

Istanbul 64, 207, 323, 373

Italy 52, 81, 84, 110, 133, 135, 141, 143, 156, 162, 165, 167, 171, 172, 177, 196, 198, **202-203**, 208, 237, 239, 275, 283,

Rothschild family 119, 133

Rovno 168

Rubenstein, Richard 192

Rubinowicz, D. 103

Rublee, George 340

Rudashevski, Yitzhak 102

Rudninkai Forest 227, 298, 299

Rumbuli Forest 233, 331

Rumkowski, Mordechai Chaim 57, 214, 246, 247, **340-341**

Russia (see Soviet Russia)

Ruthenia 86

Rwanda 193

S

Saar 159, 235

Sachs, Nelly 243, 244

Sachsenhausen 44, 53, 82, 104, 173, 182, 195, 228, 229, 263, 283, **343-344**

Safran, Alexander 66, 336

Saint Gallen 173, 174

Saint Louis **344-345**

Salaspils 233

Salonika 65, 171, **345-346**

Sammern, Ferdinand von 423

San Francisco 31

Sassen, Willem 115

Satu Mare 395

Sauckel, Fritz 287, 289, **346-347**, 366

Saxony 392

Schacht, Hjalmar 289, 340, **347**

Schilling, Claus 89

Schindler, Oskar 38, 135, 136, 228, 303, 333, **347-348**, 389

Schirach, Baldur von 287, 289

Schlondorff, Volker 135

Schloss 75

Schneerson, Isaac 75

Schoenberg, Arnold 274

Scholl, Hans and Sophie 429

Schroeder, Gustav 344

Schulte, Eduard 330

Schumann, Horst 35, 263

Schuschnigg, Kurt von 351

Schwarz-Bart, André 243

Scotland 61

Sdolbunov 155

Sebastian, Ludwig 124

Seckek-Drucker, Hanna 97

Segal, George 31

Serbia 76, 77, **350-351**, 442, 443, 444

Sereni, Haim Enzio 295

Vrba, Rudolph 37
Vught 74, 282
Vyhne 354, 356, 435

W

Walachia 335
Waldheim, Kurt **417**
Waldlanger 75
Walesa, Lech 112
Wallenberg, Raoul 69,
    163, 198, 250, 333,
    379, 411, **417-419**,
    420, 435
Warsaw 18, 20, 21, 31,
    56, 62, 77, 78, 81,
    88, 93, 99, 101, 102,
    103, 104, 108, 111,
    112, 117, 154, 159,
    162, 183, 193, 209,
    213, 214, 215, 216,
    218, 222, 223, 227,
    242, 243, 248, 250,
    270, 272, 293, 301,
    306, 307, 309, 310,
    317, 325, 327, 333,

334, 341, 350, 354,
    366, 372, 374, 387,
    388, 395, 396, 399,
    403, 405, 412, **420-
    424**, 431, 441, 445,
    446, 447
Warthegau 13, 76,
    308, **424**
Washington D.C. 54,
    268, 271, 274, 300,
    330, 389, 409, 410,
    412, 435
Weichert, Michael 350
Weimar **425**
Weinbacher, Karl 399
Weinberg, Jeshajahu
    410
Weinfeld, Yocheved
    33
Weiss, Peter 243
Weissmandel, Michael
    Ber 64, 356, **426**,
    435
Weissova-Hoskova,
    Helga 30

Weizmann, Chaim 80,
    426-427, 429
Weizsäcker, Ernst von
    427
Weizsäcker, Richard
    von **427**
Welles, Sumner 340
Weltsch, Robert 43
Wessel, Horst 165,
    194
Westerbork 50, 78,
    144, 280, 282,
    428
Westerweel, Joop 333,
    428-429
Wetzler, Alfred 37
Wiesel, Elie 242, 243,
    410, **430**
Wiesenthal, Simon **430-
    431**
Wilhelmina, Queen
    (the Netherlands)
    280
Wilner, Arie **431**
Wirth, Christian 48

subject index

Number in parentheses indicates the volume number

Switzerland 379-380 (3)

Tunisia 400-401 (4)

Ukraine 402-403 (4)

  Kiev 221 (2)

  Lvov 251-252 (2)

Yugoslavia 442-444 (4)

  Croatia 84 (1)

  Serbia 350 (3)

CULTURAL ACTIVITIES

Archives

  Centre de Documentation Juive
    Contemporaine ("Center of
  Contemporary Jewish
    Documentation" in France) 75

  Ringelblum, Emanuel 333-334

  United States Holocaust Memorial
    Museum 409-411 (4)

  Yad Vashem 409-411 (4)

Art

  Art in the Holocaust 29-31 (1)

  Art of the Holocaust 31-33 (1)

Diaries

  Frank, Anne 144-146 (2)

  Holocaust 102-104 (1)

  Kaplan, Chaim Aaron 215-216 (2)

Films

  Films on the Holocaust 134-136 (2)

Literature

  Literature of the Holocaust 242-244 (2)

Music

  Music of the Holocaust (274) (3)

Writers

  Borowski, Tadeusz (Non-Jewish Polish
    writer) 62 (1)

  Glik, Hirsh 164-165 (2)

  Katznelson, Yitzhak 218-219 (2)

  Korczak, Janusz 223-224 (2)

  Levi, Primo 237-238 (2)

  Wiesel, Elie 430 (4)

EXTERMINATION SITES & METHODS

Babi Yar (near Kiev, Ukraine) 41-42 (1)

Fort Nine (Kovno) 139-140 (2)

Gas chambers, gas vans and crematoria
  151-153 (2)

NAZI TERMINOLOGY

Kindertransport ("Children's Transport") 221-222 (2)

Parachutists, Jewish 295-296 (2)

Refugees 320-321 (3)

Rescue of Children 325-327 (3)

Teheran Children 387 (4)

Va'ad ha-Hatsala ("Rescue Committee") 412 (4)

War Refugee Board 420 (4)

Working Group (Slovakia) 434-435 (4)

Youth Aliya 440 (4)

Personalities

  Bernadotte, Folke (Sweden) 54-55 (1)

  Duckwitz, Georg Ferdinand 109-110 (1)

  Hirschmann, Ira Arthur 183 (2)

  Lutz, Carl 250 (2)

  Morgenthau, Henry, Jr. 268 (3)

  Szenes, Hanna 381 (3)

  Visser, Lodewijk 416 (4)

  Wallenberg, Raoul 417-419 (4)

Rescue ships

  Dunera 110 (1)

Exodus 1947 125 (1)

Patria 299 (3)

Saint Louis 344-345 (3)

Struma 372-373 (3)

RESISTANCE,

  Jewish 327-328 (3)

  Partisans 297-299 (3)

  Slovak National Uprising 354-355 (3)

  Underground 404-405 (4)

  Warsaw Ghetto Uprising 422-424 (4)

Personalities

  Anielewicz, Mordechai 20-21 (1)

  Bielski, Tuvia 57-58 (1)

  Bonhoeffer, Dietrich 60 (1)

  Dibelius, Otto 104 (1)

  Draenger, Shimshon and Tova 108 (1)

  Fleischmann, Gisi 138 (2)

  Frankfurter, David 147 (2)

  Glasberg, Alexandre 164 (2)

  Glik, Hirsh 164-165 (2)

  Grynszpan, Herschel 174 (2)

  Hassell, Ulrich von 177-178 (2)

  Kovner, Abba 226-227 (2)

Nuremberg Trials 287-289 (3)

Trials of War Criminals 397-400 (4)

United Nations War Crimes
Commission (UNWCC) 406-
407 (4)

UNITED STATES OF AMERICA

American Friends Service Committee
(AFSC) 17 (1)

American Jewish Joint Distribution
Committee (JDC, "Joint") 17-
18 (1)

American Jewry and the Holocaust 18-
19 (1)

American Press and the Holocaust 19-
20 (1)

Bergson Group (Revisionist Zionist
Movement in U.S.) 51-52 (1)

Fort Ontario 140-141 (2)

HICEM 180 (2)

President's Advisory Committee on
Political Refugees (PACPR) 311-
312 (3)

United States and the Holocaust 407-
409 (4)

United States Holocaust Memorial
Museum 409-411 (4)

Va'ad ha-Hatsala (Rescue Committee)
412 (4)

War Refugee Board (WRB) 420 (4)

Personalities

Morgenthau, Henry, Jr. 268 (3)

Pehle, John W. 300 (3)

Roosevelt, Franklin D. 338-339 (3)

Truman, Harry S. 400 (4)

Wise, Stephen Samuel 432 (4)

VICTIMS

Children 77-79 (1)

Death Marches 93-95 (1)

Deportations 99-102 (1)

Forced labor 138-139 (2)

Gypsies 175-176 (2)

Homosexuals 194 (2)

Soviet prisoners of war 360-361 (3)

WORLD WAR II 436-438 (4)

Appeasement 26-27 (1)

Barbarossa, Operation (Nazi invasion of

acknowledgments

The Publishers wish to express their special thanks to Michael Berenbaum, Director, United States Holocaust Research Institute, United States Holocaust Memorial Museum, Washington, D.C. and Scott Miller, University Programs Coordinator, United States Holocaust Research Institute, United States Holocaust Memorial Museum, Washington, D.C.

Special thanks to Genya Markon, Director of Photo Archives, United States Holocaust Research Institute, United States Holocaust Memorial Museum and Danny Uziel, Films and Photos Department, Yad Vashem Archives for their help in supplying illustrations for these volumes.

PHOTO CREDITS

American Jewish Archives, Courtesy of the United States Holocaust Memorial Museum 105 bottom

The American Jewish Joint Distribution Committee, Inc. Courtesy of the United States Holocaust Memorial Museum photo by Al Taylor 18; 52, 85, 321

Anne Frank Stichting, Amsterdam 21 top and bottom; 103, 145

Bak, Samuel 29 right

Beit Hannah Szenes, Courtesy United States Holocaust Memorial Museum 381

Beth Hatefutsoth 16, 59 top

Bibliotheque Historique de la ville de Paris, Courtesy of the United States of the Holocaust Memorial Museum 296

Brosh, Yaakov 261

Bundesarchiv, Courtesy of the United States Holocaust Memorial Museum 63, 81, 316 bottom, 374

C. D. Ec, Milano, Courtesy of the United States Holocaust Memorial Museum 55 Central Zionist Archives, Jerusalem 125, 198 bottom, 201, 294, 348 bottom, 404

Dokumentations Archiv des Osterreichischen Wiederstand, Courtesy of the United States Holocaust Memorial Museum 124 top

Franklin D. Roosevelt Library, Courtesy of the United States Holocaust Memorial Museum 141, 339 Fritta, Bedrich 30 left

Gefen, Aba 102

Ghetto Fighters' House 6, 138, 160, 163 top and bottom, 196 bottom, 217, 295, 312–322

Harari, Isaac 149 top

Hungarian National History Museum, Courtesy of the United States Holocaust Museum 29 left, 198 top, Thomas Veres

Institute for Military History, Courtesy of the United States Holocaust Memorial Museum 360

International Museum of Photography at George Eastman House, Rochester, N.Y., Courtesy of the United States Holocaust Memorial Museum 329 bottom

The Jerusalem Publishing House, 15, 32 right, 39, 47, 70, 98, 122, 137, 143, 157, 169, 172, 202, 234, 240, 244, 269, 281, 307, 311, 336, 362, 364, 379, 401 bottom, 424, 439, 442 Jerzy Tomaszewsk, Courtesy of the United States Holocaust Memorial Museum 117

The Jewish Museum of Greece, Courtesy of the United States Holocaust Memorial Museum 171

Jewish State Museum of Lithuania, Courtesy of the United States Holocaust Memorial Museum 118

Joods Historisch Museum, Amsterdam, Courtesy of the United States Holocaust Memorial Museum 282

Kantor, Alfred 30 Right Keter Publishing House Ltd. 74

Levin, Dov 140 left, 298 top

Lourie, Esther 225

Main Commission for the Investigation of Nazi War Crimes, Courtesy of the United States Holocaust Memorial Museum 27, 155 top, 175 bottom, 318, 425,

Mordecai Ardon Estate, 32 left

Museum of Danish Resistance, Courtesy of the United States Holocaust Memorial Museum 378

Museum of Demark's Fight for Freedom, Courtesy of the United States Holocaust Memorial Museum 99

National Archives, Courtesy of the United States Holocaust Memorial Museum 58, 61 bottom; 58, 66, 67, 73 bottom; 116; 119, 149 bottom, 150, 166, 178, 238 bottom, 239 bottom, 276, 287, 291

National Archives—Kiev, Courtesy of the United States Holocaust Memorial Museum 221, 361

National Museum of Auschwitz-Birkenau, Courtesy of the United States Holocaust Memorial Museum 36 bottom right and left, photo Arnold Kramer, 73 top, 209

National Museum, Amsterdam, Courtesy of the United States Holocaust Memorial Museum 249 top

Polska Agencja Prasowa, Courtesy of the United States Holocaust Memorial Museum 266

Pfefferberg-Page, Leopold, Courtesy of the United States Holocaust Memorial Museum 347

Rijksinstituut voor Oorlogsdocumentatie, Amsterdam, Courtesy of the United States Holocaust Memorial Museum 74, 161 top, 262, 280, 415

Rosensaft, Hadassah, Courtesy of United States Holocaust Memorial Museum 51

SIB Photo Service—Moscow, Courtesy of Yad Vashem 368 top

Sifriat Poalim, Courtesy of 22 bottom, 24 bottom, 26, 46, 50, 54, 56, 57 right, 75, 100, 107, 108, 110, 141,147, 148, 150, 154, 159, 169 top, 173, 179 right, 195 top, 222 right and left, 231, 237, 268, 279 top, 283 bottom, 292, 300, 301, 304, 305 top, 309 top, 314, 324, 330, 335, 369, 372, 376, 388, 392 right and left, 394 top, 403, 417, 426, 428 top, 429, 430, 431, 432 left, 437, 445, 446

Stadt Frankfurt am Main, Judisches Museum, Courtesy of the United States Holocaust Memorial Museum 161 bottom, 162, 246, 247, 305 bottom, 308

State of Israel Government Press Office, Courtesy of the United States Holocaust Memorial Museum 20, 400, 401 top

Statni Zidovske Museum, Courtesy of the United States Holocaust Memorial Museum 34, 87 top and bottom

United States Holocaust Memorial Museum, Photo Archives 42, 43, 44, 45, 53, 57 left; 105 top 106, 124 bottom, 167 left, 175 top, 185, 187, 219, 220, 252, 271, 272 top right, 273 top left, 313 , 317, 319 bottom, 365, 375, 387, 406, 408 bottom, 409, 410, 418, 443 bottom,

Wigoder, Geoffrey, Jerusalem 22 top; 36 top; 93, 152 top and bottom, 170 bottom, 212, 214, 229 top, 239 top, 260, 272 bottom right and left, 272 top left, 273 top right, 273 bottom, 298 top, 338, 391, 414 top, 419, 447

Yad Vashem 23, 24 top; 25, 41, 48, 59 bottom; 61 top, 69, 76, 78, 90 top and bottom, 91, 92, 94, 101, 109, 111, 113, 121, 132, 134, 139, 140 right, 142, 144, 147, 148, 151, 155 bottom, 157 top, 158 top and bottom, 164, 165, 167 right, 170 top, 174, 179 left, 182, 195 bottom, 196 top, 199, 203, 204, 205, 207, 208, 213, 218, 223, 224, 226, 228, 229 bottom, 238 top, 241, 242, 245, 248, 251, 263, 270, 277, 278, 283 top, 286, 290, 297, 298 bottom, 299, 302, 309, 316 top, 328, 329 top, 331, 332, 334, 337, 340, 341, 342, 343, 345, 346, 349 top and bottom, 351, 352, 353, 355, 357 top and bottom, 359, 365 top, 366, 367, 373, 389, 390, 394, 397, 398, 402, 405, 407, 408 top, 411, 413, 414 bottom, 421, 427, 428 bottom, 432 right, 433, 434, 436, 441, 443 top

YIVO Institute for Jewish Research, Courtesy of United States Holocaust Memorial Museum 65, 249 bottom

Copy Editing: Rachel Feldman

Secretary: Shoshanna Lewis

Typesetting and Pagination: Devorah Sowalsky—The Jerusalem Publishing House

Films: Printone Ltd., Jerusalem

Printing and Binding: Mandarin Offset Ltd., Hong Kong